Jesus Trail

and Jerusalem

D1725180

Jacob Saar   Yagil Henkin

The authors of the Israel National Trail guide

Second Edition - 2019

Reviewed by Dany Gaspar

Steinhart Sharav Publishers Ltd.

Language Editor: Shulamit Berman

Any information included in this guide might not be entirely accurate and up to date and the possibility of an error can never be eliminated. The publishers can accept no responsibility for inaccuracies and omissions. Your comments however, are always appreciated. Please post your comments on the forum:

https://www.tapatalk.com/groups/israeltrail/jesus-trail-f39

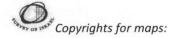 *Copyrights for maps:*

For questions please visit the forum:

https://www.tapatalk.com/groups/israeltrail/jesus-trail-f39

ISBN 978-965-42057-5-7

Table of Contents

Front cover

Left: Samakh water reservoir, Golan heights.

Middle: The Church of the Beatitudes.

Right: Scarlet crowfoot - Mt. Hermon.

Back cover: Gethsemane - The Church of all Nations.

Inside back cover:

A herd of boars on Mt. Hermon.

Mesopotamian Iris on Mt. Hermon.

Important links

Forum: www.tapatalk.com/groups/israeltrail/jesus-trail-f39/

Your comments about the guide are always appreciated. Please post them on the forum so they are immediately available to all hikers. Thank you.

www.tapatalk.com/groups/israeltrail/your-comments-about-the-guide-t610.html

GPX file: Please send a private message on the forum to the admin.

Jesus Trail

Many holy places in the world are visited by millions of people who make pilgrimages in order to draw closer to God. But there is really only one Holy Land and that is the Land of Israel, where God showed the world how to live in peace according to his commandments. *The great poet Goethe said: "Who wishes to understand the poet must go to the poet's land."* Similarly, hiking the land of Jesus is a way of understanding the Lord.

The Jesus Trail provides pilgrims with the only real opportunity to follow in the footsteps of Jesus. Marking of the trail was completed in honor of the visit of Pope Benedict XVI to the Holy land in May 2009. You will visit the Basilica of the Annunciation and Mount Precipice in Nazareth. Pope Benedict XVI delivered a mass on Mount Precipice during his visit to the Holy Land in the presence of more than 40,000 believers.

From Nazareth the trail continues to Zippori, the magnificent city built by Herod Antipas. In Cana the trail passes the wedding church where Jesus turned water into wine. John 2:11: *"This, the first of his miraculous signs, Jesus performed at Cana in Galilee. He thus revealed his glory, and his disciples put their faith in him."*

After hiking an ancient Roman road you will arrive at the Horns of Hattin, site of the famous Battle of Hattin, which was fought in 1187 between the Crusader Kingdom of Jerusalem and Saladin. Descending from the Horns of Hattin you will pass the tomb of Nabi Shu'ayb - the biblical prophet Jethro - a central figure in the Druze religion. From Mount Arbel you will enjoy a magnificent view of the Sea of Galilee, Tabgha, the Mount of Beatitudes and Capernaum. In Tabgha the trail leads to the Church of the Multiplication, situated at site where Jesus fed more than 5000 people with five loaves of bread and two fish. *Matthew 14:19, 21: "And he directed the people to sit down on the grass. Taking the five loaves and the two fish and looking up to heaven, he gave thanks and broke the loaves. The number of those who ate was about five thousand men, besides women and children."*

Overlooking Tabgha, the Mount of Beatitudes where Jesus delivered the Sermon of the Mount is your next stop on the Jesus Trail. Here more than 200,000 believers attended Pope John Paul II's mass during his visit to the Holy Land in 2000. Your next destination is the splendid Domus Galilaeae, built on a hill just above the Mount of Beatitudes. The hike along the Sea of Galilee passes the Church of the Primacy of St. Peter and continues on to Capernaum, home of St. Peter and the site where the first four disciples, James, John, Peter and Andrew were chosen. On the south side of the Sea of Galilee, while hiking the Israel National Trail you will come to the Yardenit baptismal site on the River Jordan. A day and a half later you will climb Mount Tabor, believed to be the site of the Transfiguration. *Luke 9:30: "Two men, Moses and Elijah, appeared in glorious splendor, talking with Jesus."* The visit of Pope Paul VI to the Holy Land in January 1964 is commemorated on Mt. Tabor. From Mount Tabor the trail arrives back in Nazareth.

No hike of the Jesus Trail is complete without a visit to Jerusalem. You can hike the Israel National Trail (INT) from the Sea of Galilee to Jerusalem, or take a bus and complete the pilgrimage in Jerusalem. The final stage of the pilgrimage starts in Ein Kerem. The Church of the Visitation in Ein Kerem is your first visiting site. It was built over the site where St. John the Baptist's parents lived. In the nearby Even Sapir village you can visit the St. John in the desert church and monastery. From Ein Kerem it is a short hike to Jerusalem. From the Hebron road it is only ten kilometers to Bethlehem and the Church of the Nativity. At the southwest corner of the Old City of Jerusalem the trail passes just minutes from the Room of the Last Supper. From there you will continue to Mt. Olives and Gethsemane. Before entering the Old City you will visit Mary's Tomb. The trail ends at the Via Dolorosa and the Holy Sepulchre.

Each year millions of people visit the Holy Places. You will be among those who have truly followed in the footsteps of Jesus.

Preface

Please read the entire guide and study the maps before you start planning your trip.

Hike description

The header of each day contains: The starting point, the end point and the length in kilometers (1.6 km = 1 mi). The length is rounded up to the next kilometer. The second line includes the relevant map number(s), how much water to carry, and places to refill along the route. The hiking profile includes the height in meters above sea level, length of the day in kilometers, and few way points along the day. The hike description is printed in a regular font, starting each day at (0.0, meters). Numbers in parentheses indicate the distance in kilometers from the beginning of the day, and the height in meters above or (-) below sea level of the way point.

Water and Food

In the northern part of the country you should fill about 3 liters of water in the morning and refill during the day if necessary. Water is available in villages, kibbutzim, towns, gas stations and other places along the trail. If you plan on hiking longer distances than recommended in the guide, you will require more water. On hot days you should carry more water, up to 5 liters a day. The amount of drinking water recommended for each day's hike is included at the beginning of the daily hike description. Weather conditions and temperatures below 30°C have been taken into consideration for calculating how much water you will need. The recommended length of the hike and the landscape (ascents, flat land, etc.) and a load not exceeding 15 kg/person including water and food, are also factors that determine the amount of water to carry. **Caution**: Water used for agricultural purposes cannot be used for drinking. Food can be bought in every village on the way.

When to hike?

Spring is the best time of year for the trek. The weather is mild at this time of the year and spring blossoms are splendid. Winters in Israel are relatively mild. However, in winter you will experience some delays due to rainy weather. Fall, from September to early December, is also a good season for hiking. Although the summer is hot and is the least recommended season, you can start hiking very early in the morning, at sunrise or even earlier. At about 10:00 find some shade, rest until 15:00-16:00 when the temperatures drop, and then you can continue the hike until sunset. Keep informed about weather conditions and adapt your schedule accordingly.

Get in shape

Start your preparations before you plan to arrive in Israel. Put on your new hiking shoes and hit the trails and sidewalks in your neighborhood. After a few weeks, when blisters are no longer a hazard, fill your backpack with a load of at least 10 kilos, and continue with your daily walking routine. My preparations included a 7-km walk in 1 hour without the backpack. I did this for 2-3 weeks, 4 times a week. In addition, I made two weekend trips of 15 kilometers with my fully loaded backpack, and it did the job for me. There are many other ways to prepare yourself physically, both in the gym and outside.

Hike and rest

It is recommended that you take a short break of 10-15 minutes every hour. Once a week take a full day off. This hiking routine prevents injuries due to fatigue.

How do I know I'm not lost?

It's not easy to get lost. Just follow the trail markers all the way. A few simple rules of thumb: If you don't see trail markers for more than 5 minutes, look for one. There are very few reasons for not spotting a trail marker: Either you took a wrong turn, you missed a few markers because you were enjoying the view, or a few markers were covered by spring blossoms. If you can't find the markers, go back to the last place you saw one, look at the map, and make sure you know where you are.

Your backpack

Every experienced hiker is aware of the problems associated with carrying too much weight. After all, you cannot carry less than 4 liters/day of water on hot days, and food is important too. Reducing the weight of your fully loaded backpack becomes a matter of packing a small toothpaste, a small bar of soap or only half of one, or using ultralight gear. The first rule is: Make sure your backpack is as light as possible. The second rule is: Don't make it too heavy. The third rule: Oh well, it's the same as the first two. **Switchblade knives** are not allowed. They will be confiscated by police officers if found.

National holidays in Israel

Most stores and supermarkets are closed on Saturdays and holidays. On Fridays and holiday eves, stores are open until 2-4 p.m. Restaurants, coffee shops, cinemas, theaters and shopping centers outside cities and towns are open on Saturdays and holidays except on Yom Kippur, when everything is closed. Passover and Sukkot are 7-8 days long holidays. Only the first and the last days are considered official holidays. Here are the official holidays until 2021:

Holiday	2019	2020	2021
Passover	April 20-26	April 9-15	Mar 28-Apr 3
Independence day	May 9	April 29	April 15
Shavuot	June 9	May 29	May 17
Rosh Hashanah	Sept 30, Oct. 1	Sept. 19, 20	Sept 7, 8
Yom Kippur	October 9	September 28	Sept 16
Sukkot	October 14-21	October 3-10	Sept 21-28

Insurance

Don't leave home without it, it's not just your AMEX, but more important it is your **Medical Insurance**. Make sure it covers every emergency. In case of an accident or any other mishap, contact the police by dialing **100** (police). If necessary they will alert an emergency rescue unit. Please make sure that all such eventualities, including transportation to hospitals, are covered by your medical insurance.

Weather

For the daily weather forecast in Israel check: http://www.israelweather.co.il

Money issues

Credit cards are accepted almost everywhere. For some services you have to pay cash: Taxis, a few B&Bs and some low-cost accommodations. Withdrawing cash is mostly from ATMs. If for some reason the ATM doesn't accept your credit card and you are in a town or city, look for a bank or a post office. Daily exchange rates can be found here:

http://www.boi.org.il/en/Markets/ExchangeRates/Pages/Default.aspx

Cell phones and emergency calls

US and European cell phones can be used overseas if they are quad-band GSM phones. Ask your service provider. It's cost effective to rent a cell phone overseas, where incoming calls are free, and you have prepaid minutes while traveling. If you have rented a cellular phone with rechargeable minutes, make sure you have sufficient minutes before you start hiking. If you don't bring your cellular phone, you can rent one at Ben Gurion airport. In case of emergency call **100** (police).

Hospitals: Tiberias (Poriya): 04-665221, Zfat (Ziv) 04-6828811, Jerusalem (Hadassa) 02-6777222 or Sha'arei Tzedek 02-6555111.

From Ben-Gurion airport to Nazareth

Take a train (05:00-23:20 every 40 minutes) to Tel Aviv, or a train to Haifa. From Tel Aviv central bus station to Nazareth, take bus number 823 or 826. From Haifa central train station, bus number 331 to Nazareth. From Haifa's Lev Hamifratz train station, take bus number 332 to Nazareth. For train schedules and fares, check at: http://www.rail.co.il/EN. For bus schedules: https://www.bus.co.il and click the English tab. There is no bus or train service on Saturdays and holidays.

Taxi: When you take a taxi always ask the driver to turn on the meter. It is cheaper than a fixed-price ride. You should only settle on a fixed rate for long distances of over 30 km. For taxi within Nazareth contact: 04-6555105, 04-6081000 or 04-6555536.

No litter policy

A no-litter policy is enforced in nature preserves. Disposing of garbage is allowed only where litter collection tanks are available. Take your litter with you. Get rid of your garbage when you get to a place with litter collection tanks.

Short dictionary

East - Mizrach. **West** - Ma'arav. **North** - Tzofon. **South** - Darom. **Right** - Yemin. **Left** - Smol. **Straight** – Yashar. The word **Forest** (on maps) is a translation of the Hebrew word Ya'ar. The forest can be as small as 1 sq^2 km or a larger forested area.

Be'er - Well (of water)	**Ma'ale** - Ascent
Bevakasha - Please	**Me'ara / Me'arot** – Cave / Caves
Biq'a - Valley	**Mitzpe** - Observation point
Biq'at - Valley of	**Nahal** - Creek, stream
Ein/Ayun - Spring (of water) / Arabic	**Nahar** - River
Gadol - Large	**Rama** - Plateau
Giv'a - Hill	**Sherutim** - Restroom, Toilet
Har - Mountain	**Shvil** - Trail

11

Hirba (H.)- Ruin of an old place.	Tel - A mound. Remains of an ancient settlement.
Hirbot - Plural of Hirba	Toda - Thank you
Kama Ze Ole? - How much does it cost?	Tzomet - Road crossing
Kama? - Abbreviation of Kama Ze Ole?	Tzuk - Cliff
Kfar - Village	"KH" - The two letters combined are pronounced like the letter J in Spanish.
Katan - Small	Wadi - Dry streambed, arroyo.

Day 1: A Day in Nazareth

Map: Old city of Nazareth.

Luke 1:26-27: In the sixth month the angel Gabriel was sent from God to a city of Galilee named Nazareth, to a virgin betrothed to a man whose name was Joseph, of the house of David. And the virgin's name was Mary.

Nazareth is not cited in either the Old Testament or the Talmud. Josephus Flavius, a 1st century Romano-Jewish historian, referred to Sepphoris in his writings but made no mention of Nazareth. It must have been a small and unimportant place at the time. Nathanael asked Philip, *John 1:46: "Nazareth? Can anything good come from there?"* There were good geographical reasons for his question. The ancient Via Maris linking Syria and Egypt passed east of Mount Tabor and about 10 miles east of Nazareth.

Today Nazareth is the largest Arab city in Israel, with more than 70,000 inhabitants (2010), 70% of them Moslems and 30% Christians. Nazareth is an economic, political and cultural center for the Arabs in Israel. Nearby Natzeret Illit is mostly Jewish, with more than 40,000 inhabitants. The main tourist attractions are located in the old city of Nazareth. The streets of Nazareth are numbered.

The Basilica of Annunciation

Many grottoes and wine and olive presses dating from the Stone Age have been found in the area of the Basilica of Annunciation, proving that the district was inhabited during that period, and people engaged in agriculture. The

Basilica of Annunciation is built over several ancient churches, the earliest dating from the 4th century, and reported by a pilgrim from Piacenza at about 570 CE. The second church was built during the Crusader era but was never completed. In 1739, under Ottoman rule, a new church was constructed. This church was completely demolished in 1954 to allow for the construction of the current basilica, which was completed in 1969. The main entrance is decorated with sculptures representing scenes from the Old and New Testaments. It is the largest church in the Middle East. Its dome is 55 meters high. Open daily from 08:00-17:00.

The Synagogue Church

Isaiah 61(1):"The Spirit of the Sovereign Lord is on me, because the Lord has anointed me to proclaim good news to the poor. He has sent me to bind up the brokenhearted, to proclaim freedom for the captives and release from darkness for the prisoners."

The Synagogue Church stands at the site where, according to tradition, Jesus stood to proclaim the words of the prophet Isaiah. It was built during the Crusader period and since 1771 the Greek Catholics have taken care of it. The church is located just a few minute walk into the old market. Open: Mon-Sat: 09:00-12:30; Mon, Tue, Thu, Fri 14:00-18:00. Sun - closed.

Greek Orthodox Diocese

Open: Mon-Sat 08:00-16:00 Sun: Closed. Tel: 04-6554914. It is located on the northeast side of the old city. Please dress modestly and speak softly.

This is the residency of the Greek-Orthodox Bishop of Nazareth. The building is located in the old city, was established in 1860 by Bishop Nippon. Three years later a church was established there as well. The building is shaped in a U shape and surrounded with walls like the rest of the convents. Remains of 2000 years old traditional residential caves were found under this building, probably from Roman times. The visit of the caves is recommended. In addition, this is where the Greek Orthodox community's court of law is located. The nearby square is called "The Bishop Square".

Mensa Christi Church

In the 17th century visiting pilgrims left marks on the rock where, according to tradition, Jesus ate with his disciples after the Resurrection. The huge rock is now located inside the church. Initially the Franciscans built a chapel at the site at the end of the 18th century, but it was rebuilt in 1861 in its present form. The church is not open for regular visits but the keys are with a family living across from the church. They will be glad to give you the key. A small gratuity is welcome. The church is located on 6126 street.

The White Mosque

The White Mosque, located in the center of the Old City, is the oldest Mosque in Nazareth. It was built in the early 19th century. The building was funded by Egyptian ruler Suleiman Pasha and its construction was supervised by Sheikh Abdulla Al-Fahum. Sheikh Abdulla chose white to represent purity, light, and peace between the various faiths of Nazareth. His tomb can be seen in the courtyard of the mosque, Old photos of Nazareth are on display in the mosque.

Mount Precipice

Luke 4:29-30: "And they rose up and drove him out of the town and brought him to the brow of the hill on which their town was built, so that they could throw him down the cliff. But passing through their midst, he went away."

Mount Precipice is located south of Nazareth, overlooking the Jezreel valley and Mount Tabor. It can be reached by taxi or on foot. If you prefer, you can visit Mount Precipice at the end of day 12.

Nazareth Village

Based on New Testament scholarship and the most up-to-date archaeology, Nazareth Village brings to life a farm and a Galilean village, recreating Nazareth as it was 2,000 years ago in the time of Jesus. Come and meet the people and experience first-century hospitality. Step through a stone doorway into the dim interior and smell the smoke from the oil lamps. Tel: 04-6456042 www.nazarethvillage.com.

The Market

The Nazareth Market is adjacent to the Basilica of the Annunciation. Experience the colors of the fruit market and the aroma of spices. Here you can purchase a variety of religious and other souvenirs. On weekends the market becomes even more vivid when merchants from the Galilee arrive to sell their merchandise. On the edge of the Old City, not far from Mary's well, is the Galilee Mill or El-Babour. The mill was built by the Wagner family of the Templar movement at the end of the 19th century to provide grinding and storage services for the city's farmers. The store has over 1000 species of spices and herbs.

Other attractions and tourist information

For all other attractions, accommodations and restaurants, please visit www.nazarethinfo.org.

Day 2: Nazareth to Cana - 15 km

Maps: Old City of Nazareth, maps 1, 2. Water 3 liters, refill in Zippori and in Meshad.

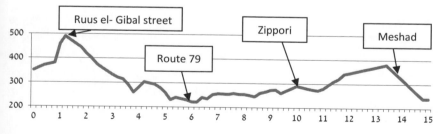

A visit to ancient Zippori is recommended. Allow at least 2 hours. If you wish to return from Zippori National Park to Nazareth, you can do so by taxi. From Meshad junction you can take a bus back to Nazareth.

Start the day at the Basilica of the Annunciation (0.0, 350). From the Basilica enter the market and go up 6152 street. The trail is marked with orange dots. Turn right by the white mosque (0.3, 360) onto 6133 street. Turn left onto 6112 street (0.4, 370). After a mild ascent continue on 6126 street. Pass by the **Mensa Christi Church** (0.8, 380). The ascent becomes steep when you climb the steps that end on 5004 street, the Salesian Street (1.0, 440). Turn left and continue the ascent, passing the Salesian Sisters monastery on your left (1.1, 450). The trail markers are now the regular ones. At the top of the ascent turn left (1.1, 490) and you will see a panoramic view extending south to Haifa.

Turn left at a roundabout and continue down. At the next roundabout turn right and down. The trail turns down & left (1.8, 445). By the last house of street you hike a rocky hill, goes down, cross a wadi (4.0, 260) and climbs a hill. At the top of the short assent turn right and hike by a pine tree grove. Turn sharply left (4.7, 295). Cross a road (5.3, 230) and following a short ascent arrive at route 79 (5.8, 230). Cross carefully the busy road and continue by the entry road to Zippori. Turn left off the paved road. It winds east of Zippori village. The trail turns right & down and crosses a paved road (9.4, 260). Turn left and arrive at the gate of Zippori National Park (9.9, 290).

Zippori (Sepphoris) National Park

April to September: 08:00-17:00, October to March: 08:00-16:00, Fee. There is a snack bar, picnic area and restrooms. Tel: 04-6568272.

When Herod the Great was consolidating his power over the country early in his reign (37 BCE), Zippori fell to him without a battle. After Herod's death (4 BCE) a rebellion broke out against the Romans, but it was quelled when Zippori was destroyed by the Roman governor Varus. Herod Antipas restored the town so beautifully that Josephus Flavius described it as "the ornament of all Galilee." Later, Rabbi Judah Hanassi moved the Sanhedrin from Bet She'arim to Zippori, where he redacted the Mishnah in 220 CE. The sages of Zippori also contributed to the Jerusalem Talmud, which was completed in the 4th century CE. Christians and Jews lived together here from the 5th century on. The presence of a small Jewish community during the middle Ages is indicated by a letter found in the Cairo in the 10th century. The Crusaders believed that Ann and Joachim, the parents of Mary, mother of Jesus, lived here. Remains of the church they built commemorating St. Ann can still be seen.

A Crusader fortress, rebuilt in the 18th century by Daher al-Omar, the Bedouin ruler of the Galilee, stands at the top of a hill. The village at that time was called Safouriyeh. The 4,500-seat Roman theatre, which has been partially restored, affords a beautiful view of the Galilee Mountains and the Beit Netofa valley. Other attractions include a Talmudic-era residential quarter; the Crusader fortress; the restored 3rd century villa housing a magnificent mosaic depicting scenes from the life of Dionysus, the god of wine; and the hauntingly beautiful "Mona Lisa of the Galilee." The synagogue with its magnificent mosaic and the Nile Mosaic from the 5th century CE are also highlights, as is the 250-meter-long, 1st century CE underground water system, with a capacity of 5,000 cubic meters.

After the visit take the trail straight and east from the gate, and a few hundred meters further on the Jesus Trail joins the Israel National Trail (INT) (10.3, 260). The markers are now red. Make a right turn onto a mild ascent (11.0, 270) in a grove of pine trees. Arrive at a dirt road and turn left (11.8, 340), and climb to Meshad. By the cemetery turn left (13.5, 380) and at the main mosque the INT goes right but you turn left and down on Jesus Trail (13.7, 360). *If you want to return to Nazareth by bus, turn right on the INT and hike down until you arrive at the Meshad crossing.* Continue down and east and exit Meshad (14.3, 300) among olive groves in the direction of Cana. Arrive at the main street of Cana (14.8, 240). Turn left and after about 100 meters make a right turn into an alley (14.9, 240) and continue past the sun dial toward the Wedding Church (15.4, 230).

Cana (modern name Kafr Kanna) is a Galilean town five miles northeast of Nazareth. Its' population of 21,000 includes both Muslims and Christians. Long revered as the site of Jesus' first miracle of turning water into wine at a wedding, Kafr Kanna has historical support for its authenticity as ancient Cana. The Catholic Encyclopedia of 1914, in a tradition dating back to the 8th century, identifies Cana with the town of Kafr Kana. A few recent scholars *have suggested alternatives, including the village of Kenet-el-Jalil, also known as Khirbet Kana, a few kilometers further north.*

The Franciscan Wedding Church at Cana was built in 1881. It is fronted by a courtyard. The facade has angel figures and is flanked by two bell towers over an arcaded narthex. Inside, the church is on two levels. The upper church has a chapel surmounted by a simple dome. In the nave just before the stairs is a fragment of a Byzantine mosaic dating from the 5th century that preserves the name of the donor in Aramaic: "In memory of the pious Joseph, son of Tanhum, son of Bota and of his children who made this table, may it be for them a blessing, Amen." The lower church has a chapel and a small museum with artifacts from the site, including a winepress, a plastered cistern and vessels of various dates. One old jar is said to be one of the six used for the miracle. Open: Mon-Sat 08:00-12:00; 14:00-18:00. Sun closed.

Opposite the Franciscan church is a beautiful Greek Orthodox Church, which is not always open. Two 13th century capitals are displayed nearby.

Spend the night at the Cana guest house, located minutes from the Wedding Church. Tel: 04-651-7186 - Sami. www.canaguesthouse.com.

Day 3: Cana to Lavi - 17 km

Maps: 2, 3. Water: 4 liters, refill at the Golani junction. There is no grocery store in Lavi, carry food for two days.

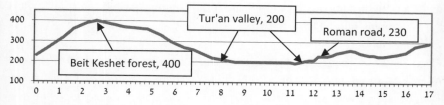

From the Golani junction you can return to Nazareth by bus. There is a MacDonald's at the Golani junction on the north side of route 77. On the south side of route 77 by the Golani junction there is a gas station, convenience store and a restaurant.

Start the day in Cana (0.0, 230) climb east and exit the village (1.6, 360). The paved road turns into a dirt road. You are now hiking in the Beit Keshet forest reserve. The trail turns slightly right (2.6, 400). Arrive at a paved road which is a green trail and turn left (4.8, 360). Go down along the paved road and turn left on a red trail (5.4, 330). The trail narrows and descends overlooking the beautiful Tur'an valley. Leave the red trail after a few hundred meters and turn right and east (5.7, 300). Continue until you reach the paved road that you left earlier (6.7, 260). Turn left and continue along the road. The trail markers are now green. In a pine grove on your right is a small picnic area with a few tables (7.6, 220). The area was dedicated in honor of the queen of Holland.

Turn right, and the paved road turns into a dirt road. **The Gospel trail** joins from the right (8.4, 200). *The Gospel trail is an initiative of the Israel ministry of tourism.* Cross another paved road and on your left is a small snack bar (8.6, 200). *The sandwiches and prices are excellent. Joshua is the owner. Open: Sun-Thu 07:00-19:00.* The markers are orange now. Continue east on a dirt road and turn left along an old road with old electrical poles dating from the 50's (10.4, 200). Pass by a pumping station and continue north to cross route 77 on Golani junction. The trail turns right, crosses route 65 on an overpass and arrives at the Golani Brigade memorial center and museum (12.3, 210).

The Golani brigade, established on February 22, 1948, has taken part in all of Israel's wars since 1948. The museum is open Sun-Thu 09:00-16:00; Fri 09:00-13:00. The displays are in Hebrew. There is a MacDonald's next to the entrance to the museum.

Continue east and by the Eucalypti trees grove the remains of an ancient Roman road are visible. (12.5, 230).

The Roman road linked Acre on the Mediterranean with Tiberias on the Sea of Galilee. Route 77 in the Tur'an valley parallels the ancient Roman road. Another good example of a modern road that follows a similar path to a Roman road is the one from Ashkelon on the Mediterranean to Jerusalem. Distances on Roman roads were measured by milestones. Several milestones from the Roman era can still be seen on the ancient road from Ashkelon to Jerusalem. The Romans utilized a vast network of roads to control and protect

19

their empire. The main roads were for public and military use. There were also private and agricultural roads, and the regional roads were dirt roads. The road here is of the first type.

Turn right and east and hike toward Kibbutz Lavi. You will hike next to a power line (13.2, 260). Turn right away from the power line (14.2, 240) and after a short and very mild descent arrive at Lavi cemetery and a Holocaust memorial (15.0, 230). There is water in the cemetery.

The Holocaust memorial commemorates the parents and relatives of members of Kibbutz Lavi, which is a religious community established in 1949 by young immigrants mostly from the UK. They were refugees from Nazi Germany who were part of the Kindertransport, a rescue mission undertaken shortly before the Second World War to save Jewish children from the Nazis. The UK took in almost 10,000 children.

To get to the Illaniya B&B turn right by the cemetery and hike south until you reach route 77. Contact the Illaniya B&B from the Lavi junction and make sure they will pick you up. The Lavi hotel is on the grounds of the kibbutz. If you prefer you can camp in the area or in the Lavi forest in a designated camping area east of the Golani junction.

Turn left from the cemetery to the north. Turn right and east (15.6, 240) and go uphill, crossing a gate in a cattle fence, until the trail passes by the rear gate of the kibbutz (16.7, 290). Turn right onto the road that leads to the hotel. There are signs pointing to the hotel. Kibbutz Lavi is a Jewish religious community.

Day 4: Lavi to Moshav Arbel - 15 km

Maps: 3, 4. Water 4 liters, refill in Nabi Shua'yb.

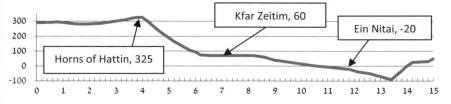

If you spend the night in Illaniya B&B ask the owner to drop you off at the rear gate of Kibbutz Lavi, which is not far from the Lavi hotel. There is a B&B in Kfar Zeitim and in Moshav Arbel.

Start the day at the rear gate of kibbutz Lavi (0.0, 290). From the gate take a dirt road that joins the trail by the Lavi dairy farm or go back to the trail and continue northeast passing under a power line (0.7, 295). Turn right (1.5, 280) and after passing the Lavi dairy farm turn left (1.8, 280). Pass a cattle guard and turn right onto a black trail (2.3, 285). Continue east on a mild ascent towards the Horns of Hattin. Pass a cattle grid and when you meet a blue trail turn left at the foot of the Horns of Hattin. Climb the hill on your left for a magnificent panorama of the area (4.0, 325).

On July 4th, 1187 Saladin of the Ayyubid dynasty fought and defeated the Crusader Kingdom of Jerusalem under the leadership of Guy of Lusignan and Raymond III of Tripoli. One day earlier the Crusaders had left Zippori to face Saladin's advance forces. At midday they arrived at the village of Tur'an, where water was available, Guy had decided to march towards the town of Tiberias, that had been taken by Saladin. The Crusaders could not cover the distance of 14 km due to continuous attacks by Saladin's cavalry. Lacking water and supplies, they were forced to stop in the area of Hattin. The next day they were defeated and suffered very heavy casualties. Most of the Crusaders, some 17,000 in all, lost their lives, while Saladin's forces suffered only minor loses. Guy of Lusignan was captured along with several other leaders. He was brought to Syria and released the following year.

Mount Arbel and the Arbel valley are visible to the east from the Horns of Hattin. Continue northwest on a blue trail. The trail goes down on a steep and rocky descent that becomes moderate for a short distance (4.4, 270). The trail veers until it arrives at the entry road to Nabi Shu'ayb (5.2, 165). Turn left to visit the holy site.

Nabi Shu'ayb (The prophet Jethro), is a central figure in the Druze religion. The tomb of Nabi Shu'ayb has been a site of annual pilgrimage for the Druze for centuries. The first mention of the tomb dates back to the 12th century CE, and the Druze have held religious festivals there for centuries. According to Druze tradition, the imprint of Shu'ayb's left foot (da'sa) can be seen on the grave. Pilgrims visiting the site pour oil into the imprint, and then rub the oil over their body in order to be blessed with good fortune. The Druze customarily had no fixed date for their annual pilgrimage, which generally occurred sometime in the spring. When the Israeli government granted official recognition of the pilgrimage as a Druze religious holiday, the dates were standardized, and the event now takes place between April 25 and April 28. During the festivities, mass celebrations are held at Nabi Shu'ayb, and Druze religious leaders gather there for ritual purposes and to discuss religious questions.

The five-colored Druze flag was designed to distinguish the Druze Islamic sect from other sects. There are many interpretations for this flag, but the main one is that it represents Fatimah, her father (Muhammad), her husband, and her two sons. Other interpretations of the five colors are: Red is for courage, bravery and love. Yellow is knowledge, wisdom, enlightenment and wheat. Green is nature and earth. Blue signifies patience, forgiveness, sky and water. White is purity, peace and conciliation.

Nabi Shu'ayb has been expanded and renovated over time. The older section of the existing structure was built in the 1880s, after the spiritual leader of the Druze, Sheikh Muhammad Tarif, summoned an assembly of religious leaders in the community to collaborate on its construction. A delegation of high-ranking community members traveled to Syria and Lebanon to collect funds for the new construction and renovations, and the Druze of the Galilee and Mount Carmel also made considerable contributions. The chandelier in the central convention hall was designed in Syria, the glass came from Egypt, and the construction was completed by experts from Jordan.

From Nabi Shu'ayb continue on the paved road (turn right when coming down from the Horns of Hattin) east and at route 7717 turn left toward Kfar Zeitim (6.2, 75). *In Kfar Zeitim there is a B&B.* At the entrance to Kfar Zeitim (6.6, 70) continue straight on a blue trail which is dirt road, next to an olive grove. On you left you will see the ruins of the Arab village of Hittin. Make a right turn where a black trail joins from the left (8.2, 70). There is an impressive view of Mount Arbel and Mount Nitai to the east. Continue on a very mild descent along Nahal Nimerim. When you come to a fork in the dirt road make a left turn and you will pass a pumping station, Hittim (חיטים) number 3 (8.9, 40). Cross a cattle guard and arrive at another fork in the dirt road. The black trail goes left, and you make a right turn and continue on the blue trail (10.6, 0), you are at sea level now.

Cross a cattle guard and arrive at Ein Nitai (11.7, -20). This small and lovely spring is the perfect place for a break. Continue east along Nahal Arbel on the gravel road, passing few large eucalyptus trees (12.2, -40). A few hundred meters further along Nahal Arbel you will see a huge mulberry tree. Cross Nahal Arbel a few times and at the entrance to the Arbel Nature Reserve by an abandoned building (13.3, -90) make a right turn to begin the steep ascent toward Moshav Arbel. The blue trail ends above sea level at the entry road to Moshav Arbel (14.1, 25). Turn left and then turn right and follow a green trail that brings you to the ancient Arbel Synagogue (14.8, 30), that dates back to the 4th century CE. To reach Moshav Arbel take the trail that goes south from the Synagogue into Moshav Arbel (15.3, 50). *You can camp out in the area.*

Day 5: Moshav Arbel to Tabgha - 15 km

Maps: 4, 5. Water 4 liters, refill in Migdal.

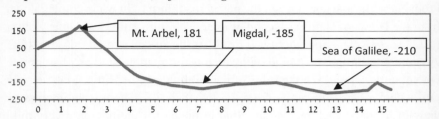

Start the day at the road to Mount Arbel, on the north side of Moshav Arbel (0.0, 50). Climb east and arrive at Mt. Arbel Park (fee) (1.5, 150). If you start early enough you can watch the sun rise over the Golan Heights and the Sea of Galilee (Kinneret). Take the black trail that leads to the top of the cliff (1.8, 181). The view towards the Kinneret, some 400 meters below, is magnificent. Mount Nitai is opposite, on the other side of the deep valley which was formed by volcanic activity.

The name Kinneret was mentioned as early as 1450 BCE by Thutmose the 3rd as one of the places he captured during his reign. The word Kinneret is derived from the Canaanite language. Later, in the Talmudic period (300-400 CE), it was known as the "Sea of Tiberias," a name which is used in Arabic بحيرة طبريا (Buheirat Tabria) and in French "Le lac de Tibériade". The Latin Name "Mare Galilaeae" is similar to the Sea of Galilee.

Descend from Mt. Arbel on the black trail that follows the path of the Israel National Trail (INT). Metal handles and cables assist you on the way down. You will pass by the Arbel Fort.

The site was inhabited as early as the Stone Age. The natural caves were expanded to include water cisterns. During the Hasmonean revolt (167-161 BCE) against Antiochus the 4th Epiphanes, the caves were used as a hiding place. The soldiers of King Herod (74-4 BCE) chased the Kanaim (Zealot) rebels who hid here.. Herod's soldiers lowered baskets from the cliff top to gain entry to the caves. During the great Jewish Revolt (66-70 CE) the Kanaim rebels in the Galilee also made use of the caves until the Romans, led by

24

Vespasian (9-79 CE) and succeeded by his son Titus (39-81 CE), ended the revolt and destroyed the Second Temple (70 CE). The Arbel Fort dates back to the 17th century, when it was used by the Druze in their revolt against the Ottoman rulers.

Continue the descent until you link up with the red trail (2.9, 40) that goes down from the west side of the Arbel cliff; you are now hiking below sea level. Arrive at Hamam, a Bedouin village of the Awarna tribe (4.5, -115). *The original families lived in 13 small villages further north in the Hula valley. In 1948 they were moved here. There is a grocery store in Hamam.* Continue towards the exit from Hamam and cross route 807 by the gas station (5.7, -165). Continue north to Migdal. Pass a small supermarket by the main entrance road to Migdal (7.1, -185). Continue north on the INT. Pass Ein Nun - the Nun spring, which is a lovely place for a break. A blue trail crosses the INT (8.7, -160).

The INT turns right and east to Nahal Amud on a black trail (10.3, -150). Cross route 90 using an underpass (11.8, -195). Continue east and arrive at the sea of Galilee (12.5, -210). Turn left and north. Pass by *Hirbat Minim national park.* Arrive at a road and turn left (13.9, -200). To the right the road enters the Sapir water pumping facility. By route 90 (14.4, -195) turn right. After a short ascent go down and crosses the access road to Pilgerhaus Tabgha (14.5, -190). *It was established in 1889 by the Lazarists, whose goal, apart from pilgrimage, was to train local Bedouins in agriculture. After 1948 the site was confiscated, and in the 1990's it was returned to the German Association for the Holy Land.* Arrive at Tabgha (14.9, -190).

There are several places to stay in the area: Migdal, Tamar camping site, Pilgerhaus Tabgha, the Mount of Beatitudes Guesthouse (2 minutes by bus from Tabgha + 0.75 km walk from the road, or hike north and uphill from Tabgha for approx. 1.5 km), Vered Hagalil and Korazim, both less than 10 minutes by bus. Please check in Accommodations for details. Buses from the Kfar Nahum junction run every 30 minutes between 07:00-20:00 and every hour after 20:00. On Friday the buses run until 17:00.

Day 6: Holy Sites on the Shore of the Sea of Galilee

Map: 5. Water 3 liters, refill in Capernaum.

If you want to visit all the holy sites on the north shore of the Sea of Galilee, it is recommended that you spend two days in the area. On the first day you will visit the Mount of Beatitudes, Tabgha, the St. Peter Primacy Church, and Capernaum. On the second day we recommend to visit the Domus Galilaeae in Korazim and the Jesus Boat in Ginosar. Both places can be reached by bus.

Mount of Beatitudes to Capernaum - 12 km

There is no hiking trail from the Domus Galilaeae to the Mount of Beatitudes. The area is blocked by a barbed-wire cattle fence. Take a bus if you are not staying at the Mount of Beatitudes hostel. The buses on route 90 run every 30 minutes or so. There is a bus station on route 90, at the entry road leading to the monastery and church. From the bus station hike east and arrive at the entrance to the Mount of Beatitudes church and monastery (~1 km). The only descent of the day is from Mount of Beatitudes to Tabgha an elevation change of ~100 meters. The rest of the day is hiking along the shores of the Sea of Galilee.

Start the day on the Mount of Beatitudes (0.0, -90). After visiting the Church take a non-marked trail (dirt road) down and south toward Tabgha and the Sea of Galilee. Just before arriving at route 87 on your right there is a tiny cave with a bench (1.4, -180). Take a break and enjoy the view of the Sea of Galilee. Go down by way of the metal stairs and carefully cross route 87 (1.5, -190). Turn right and continue on the sidewalk to Tabgha (2.0, -190). After visiting Tabgha turn back (east) and visit the Church of the Primacy of St. Peter (2.5, -190). Continue east to visit Capernaum. Turn right at the entrance road to Capernaum (4.4, -195) and arrive at a gate (5.0, -200). After visiting Capernaum return to route 87 (5.5, -195), turn right and continue east along route 87. Turn right (6.4, -195) and arrive at the lovely seven Apostles Greek Orthodox church (7.2, -210). Hike back to Tabgha along route 87 and arrive to route 90 (11.7, -190). Take a bus back to where you plan to spend the night.

Mount of Beatitudes

Open: Daily 08:00-11:30; 14:00-16:30. Allow up to one hour. Free.

Matthew 5:1-3: "Now when Jesus saw the crowds, he went up on a mountainside and sat down. His disciples came to him, and he began to teach them: Blessed are the poor in spirit, for theirs is the kingdom of heaven."

Located on a hill overlooking the Sea of Galilee and Tabgha, the Mount of Beatitudes is, according to tradition, the site where Jesus delivered the most famous sermon of all times: The Sermon on the Mount. It is questionable whether this is the exact location where he stood and spoke to his disciples, but considering that Jesus lived in Capernaum and the area is not mountainous, this hill is a likely site for the Sermon on the Mount. Remains of a 4th century Byzantine church have been found here. Parts of a cistern and a monastery are still visible.

In 1907 the area was purchased by the *"Associazione Nazionale per Soccorrere i Missionari Italiani"*, the National Association for Assistance to Italian Missionaries, founded in 1886. The church was built in 1938. The architect was Antonio Barluzzi (1884-1960), who designed many religious institutions in the Holy Land. The shape of the church is octagonal, to represent the eight beatitudes. The lower walls are encased in marble veneer and the dome is covered in gold mosaic. The main attraction is the cool, quiet garden overlooking the Sea of Galilee. Here, where Jesus conducted his ministry, is an excellent place to contemplate some of the best-known Christian teachings.

Tabgha and the Church of the Multiplication

Open: Mon-Fri 08:00-17:00; Sat: 08:00-15:00. Sun closed. Allow half an hour. Free.

Tabgha is traditionally believed to be the site of the miracle of the multiplication of the loaves and fishes. The story is found in all four gospels. The name is derived from the Greek *Heptapegon* ("seven springs"). A Church of the Feeding of the Five Thousand was first built here circa 350. The church was small (16m x10m) and on a slightly different orientation than the later versions. After visiting the church in the 380s, the Spanish pilgrim Egeria wrote:

"By the sea is a grassy field with plenty of hay and many palm trees. By them are seven springs, each flowing strongly. And this is the field where the Lord fed the people with the five loaves and two fishes. In fact the stone on which the Lord placed the bread has now been made into an altar. People who go there take away small pieces of the stone to bring them prosperity, and they are very effective."

The church was significantly enlarged around 480, when the splendid floor mosaic was added. The mosaics were repaired in the 6th century but the church was destroyed around 700 CE. In 1932 the site was bought and excavated by the Deutsche Verein vom Heilige Lande; a protective cover was built over the mosaics in 1936. In 1982 this was replaced by the modern Church of the Multiplication of the Loaves and Fishes that stands today and is a faithful reconstruction of the original.

Church of the Primacy of Peter

Open: Daily: 08:00-17:00. Allow half an hour. Free.

Matthew 16: 18-19: And I tell you that you are Peter and on this rock I will build my church, and the gates of Hades will not overcome it. I will give you the keys of the kingdom of heaven; whatever you bind on earth will be bound in heaven, and whatever you loose on earth will be loosed in heaven.

The Church of the Primacy of Peter is a Franciscan chapel located at Tabgha, commemorating Jesus' reinstatement of Peter. At the base of the chapel walls on the west end, the walls of the late 4th-century church are clearly visible on three sides. Like the early church, the altar of the modern chapel incorporates a large portion of the stone "table of Christ" (Latin: *Mensa Christi*). This is where Jesus is believed to have served his disciples a breakfast of fish after they landed on shore *(John 21:9)*. On the lake side of the church are the rock-cut steps mentioned by Egeria as the place "where the Lord stood."

Capernaum

Open: Daily 08:00-16:30. Allow 1 hour. Fee: NIS 3.

Matthew 4:12-13: "When Jesus heard that John had been put in prison, he returned to Galilee. Leaving Nazareth, he went and lived in Capernaum, which was by the lake in the area of Zebulun and Naphtali."

The site of the ancient fishing village of Capernaum (Hebrew: *Kfar Nahum*, the Village of Nahum) is located 2.5 kilometers northeast of Tabgha. The town is first mentioned in the New Testament, where it figures prominently in the Gospel narratives as the place where Jesus lived during much of his ministry in the Galilee. It was here that Jesus "cured many who were suffering from diseases," and also "cast out many devils" in those possessed. In 381, the pilgrim Egeria said she visited *"the synagogue where the Lord cured a man possessed by a devil. The way in is up many stairs, and it is made of dressed stone."* The synagogue at Capernaum probably dates from the 4th century CE. The ornately carved, white building stones of the synagogue stand out prominently among the smaller, plain blocks of local black basalt used for the town's other buildings, which are almost all residential.

Several of the Apostles - Peter and his brother Andrew, James son of Zebedee and his brother John - lived in the village, where Matthew was a tax collector. Archeological evidence indicates that the town was established at the beginning of the Hasmonean Dynasty (the earliest coins found at the site date from the 2nd century BCE). The town, near the border of the province of Galilee, was situated on a branch of the *Via Maris* trade route. At the time of the Gospel narrative, Capernaum included a customs post and a small Roman garrison commanded by a centurion.

The church of Capernaum was founded on the traditional site of St. Peter's home. Closer to the shore than the synagogue, the house was in a poor area where the dry stone basalt walls would have supported only a light roof (which suits the lowering of the paralytic in Mark 2:1-12) and would not have had windows. The village, badly damaged by an earthquake in 749, was rebuilt a short distance to the northeast (near the present Greek Orthodox Church), but little is known of its subsequent history, decline and eventual abandonment sometime in the 11th century. Despite the importance of Capernaum in the life of Jesus, there is no indication of any construction during the Crusader period. A 13th-century traveler found only the huts of seven poor fishermen.

The site was "re-discovered" in 1838 by Dr. Edward Robinson, the American biblical geographer. In 1866, the British explorer Captain Charles W. Wilson identified the ruins of the synagogue, and in 1894 a portion of the ancient site was purchased by the Franciscan Custody of the Holy Land. The principal Franciscan excavations took place in 1968-84. In 1990, the Franciscans built the modern church over the site of St. Peter's house. Octagonal in shape and rather spaceship-like in appearance, it is elevated on pillars and has a glass floor, so visitors can still see the original church below. In March 2000, Pope John Paul II visited Capernaum during his visit to the Holy Land.

Seven Apostles Greek Orthodox Church

Open: Daily 08:30-17:00. Allow half an hour. Free.

The small, beautiful and picturesque Seven Apostles Greek Orthodox Church, with its pink red dome, was constructed in 1931. The walls are decorated with huge frescoes painted by Greek artists. It is the most beautiful church in the area.

Day 7: Domus Galilaeae and Jesus Boat to Migdal - 5 km

Map: 5. Water 2 liters.

Take a bus to Korazim junction. From route 90 hike east on route 8277. Turn right and arrive to Domus Galilaeae (0.5). After the visit return to route 90 and take a bus to Ginosar (1.0). Visit the Jesus Boat at the local museum (1.7). From Ginosar go back to route 90 (2.4, -175) and turn left and south. After approximately 300 meters turn right on a dirt road and continue west for another 300 meters, until you reach the Jesus trail (2.5, -180), which is also the INT. Turn left and south on the INT and arrive at Migdal (3.7, -185). Continue south until you arrive at the gas station on route 807 (5.1, -185). Before you continue the hike, it is important to take half a day off and rest.

Domus Galilaeae

Open: Mon-Sat: 09:00-12:00; 15:00-16:30. Sun: Closed. Guided tours only; allow up to 1 hour. Free.

The original project is by Kiko Argüello, a famous Spanish painter, and Carmen Hernandez, the initiators of the Neocatechumenal Way. The very beautiful project of Domus Galilaeae where Pope John Paul 2nd celebrated the Eucharist on March 24th, 2000 on the Mount of Beatitudes, is an attempt to rediscover architectural and iconographic shapes and help to reintroduce beauty into the life of the Church.

Construction began in January 1999 under the direction of an Israeli architect, Dan Mochly from Haifa, in collaboration with an Argentinean architect, Rev. Daniel Cevilan. The first terrace, the highest in reference to the lake, includes a congressional center, with all the facilities for simultaneous translations, and capable of accommodating 300 persons. In order to facilitate study and to deepen the understanding of Sacred Scripture, with special attention to the Sermon of the Mount, there is a computerized library for Biblical studies. The complex includes also a Church for Eucharistic celebrations and a Chapel of the Blessed Sacrament surmounted by a stylish chalice which refers to the passion of Christ.

The Jesus Boat museum

Open: Sun-Thu 08:00-17:00; Fri 08:00-16:00; Sat 08:00-16:00. Fee.

On January 24th, 1986, a historic archaeological discovery was made on the Galilee lake shore at Kibbutz Ginosar. The discovery rocked the world of faith, history and archaeology. Following a prolonged drought that had lowered the sea level of the lake, two fisherman brothers discovered an ancient boat. In Israel, a land blessed with a rich history and hundreds of thousands of artifacts, important discoveries occur on a fairly regular basis. This discovery was different however; there must have been something more to the story.

Experts from all over the world were brought in to establish the boat's authenticity and exact age by means of scientific methods, including three independent precision Carbon-14 dating examinations that determined the boat is dated to the time of Jesus. The boat might conceivably have been used by Jesus or one of his disciples for fishing and transportation. Word of the unprecedented discovery traveled rapidly throughout the scientific community, and to people of faith around the world. What had been found was a Bible-era artifact like no other. Some consider it to be among the top ten biblical archaeological discoveries ever made. The Jesus Boat is a one-of-a-kind actual point of contact with the exact time and place of Jesus.

From the Sea of Galilee to Jerusalem

You can continue the pilgrimage on the Israel National Trail and arrive after about 2-3 weeks and 350 kilometers in the Holy City of Jerusalem.

On your way you will visit the Yardenit baptismal site which is about a day hike from Migdal. On the following day you will climb Mt. Tabor and visit the Transfiguration Church.

When you climb *Mount Carmel* and arrive to Isfiya visit the nearby Carmelites monastery which stands at the traditional site where Elijah confronted 450 Baal prophets: *1 Kings 18:21: Elijah went before the people and said, "How long will you waver between two opinions? If the LORD is God, follow him; but if Baal is God, follow him."*

From Isfiya it's only a short ride by bus to *Haifa* and the *Bahá'í World Center*. Three days later you will hike on the Mediterranean shore at the gates of the magnificent ancient city of *Caesarea Maritima*. It was built by Herod the Great at about 25-13 BCE. *Apostle Paul* pleaded his case in Caesarea to be released from charges of inciting a riot in Jerusalem, with his preaching of the gospel. Further south pass ancient Arsuf (Phoenician name) or *Apollonia* (Hellenistic name), where the crusaders created the Lordship of Arsur 1101-1187 CE, as part of the Kingdom of Jerusalem. The vibrant city of *Tel Aviv* is the next stop on the trail. *Ancient Jaffa* is a must visit when in Tel Aviv.

From Tel Aviv you will continue the hike and after three days you will climb for two more days the Judean Mountains and arrive to *Jerusalem*.

The Israel National Trail (INT) guide includes all the topographical maps (1:50,000) of the trail is available on Amazon and on Cordee.co.uk. In Israel you will find the INT guide in major book stores: Stiematzky and Tzomet Sfarim.

Jerusalem

Hiking the Jerusalem Trail is a unique experience. The hike will take you to historic and archaeological sites, you will meet fascinating people of all religions, and you will visit one of the most exciting cities in the world. You will complete the pilgrimage at the Holy Sepulchre. Since there are so many sites on or near the trail it is impossible to describe them all in detail, so I have decided to limit them to one or two lines. Please visit www.jerusalemp3.com to download free audio tours to your mp3 player. Visit the Jerusalem city website for information about attractions, free guided tours, accommodations and events. www.jerusalem.muni.il. For English click **ENG** at the top left corner.

The trail is clearly marked outside the city. Blue trail markers are clear and wooden posts are placed along the trail. Within the city some trail markers are visible when you hike in a clockwise direction but they are somewhat difficult to discern if you are going the other way. In the section between the Hebrew University on Mount Scopus (Har Hatzofim) and Giv'at Hatakhmoshet trail markers are sparse, and the trail has not yet been marked from Giv'at Hatakhmoshet to the Chords Bridge at the exit to the city. This section is not included in the guide.

We have divided the Jerusalem hike into two days for purposes of description, but we recommend to extend the hike and take the time to visit the many interesting sites along the way in the city of Jerusalem.

Day 8: Ein Karem to Emek Refaim Street - 15 km

Maps: 6-9. You can buy water all along the trail from the entrance to Ein Karem through the end of the day.

If you've hiked from Migdal to Jerusalem on the Israel National Trail, you will arrive in Ein Karem and continue the hike from at km 3.3 of the hike description. If you came to Jerusalem by public transportation, we recommend starting day 8 in Ein Karem, at km 3.3 of the day. You can spend the night at the Rosary Sisters Guesthouse in Ein Karem, next to the Church of the Visitation or at any other location of your choice.

To get to Even Sapir take Egged bus number 27a from the central bus station on Yafo Street (06:25, and 09:50). Alternatively you can ride bus 27 that goes to Hadassah Medical Center every 15 minutes, and take a taxi to Even Sapir. It is a 3 minute ride (ask the driver to turn on the meter). You can also hike from Hadassah to Even Sapir, a 1.8 km hike on the road. From Hadassah go down on route 386 and turn left after about 100 meters.. Continue on the road until you reach Even Sapir.

To get to Ein Karem from the central bus station take Egged bus number 27 or 27a, and change at Mt. Herzl to bus number 28 or 28a (every 10-15 minutes). When you come to Ein Karem get off at the main street, turn left to Hama'ayan Street and turn right at Mary's well, by the Ein Karem Music Center. Pass the entrance to the Rosary Sisters Guesthouse and another 50 meters further you will come to the entrance road of the Visitation Church.

St. John in the Desert Monastery is 15 minute-walk in **Even Sapir**. Take the main road down to the monastery. The road makes a sharp turn to the right and 500 meters further on it makes a left turn down. Arrive at the monastery after another 700 meters. Remains of a 6th century monastery were found here. The place was rebuilt by the Crusaders. The present monastery was built in 1922. Open: Sun-Fri 08:00-12:00 14:00-17:00. Sat: 08:00-17:00. Allow 30 minutes for the visit.

Start 150 meters from the entrance to Even Sapir (615, 0.0). A steep descent down a short trail will bring you to Ein Hindak (570, 0.2). At the fork in the path take the blue trail right and north, it is the Jerusalem trail. The green trail used to be part of the Israel National Trail, do not take it. Outside of Jerusalem the trail is indicated with blue trail markers. The symbol of Jerusalem - a blue and gold sign with the emblem of a lion – accompanies you within the city and sometimes outside as well. In built up areas the city trail is indicated by blue and gold markers. Follow the dirt track. This was the ancient Roman road leading from Ein Hindak. You will see a road that joins up on the right, from the direction of the Hadassah hospital (0.6, 580). As you continue walking and pass through an old gate, the path climbs gently and then descends slightly.

On your left you will see a building above a spring, and some 200 meters further, a small building over another spring above you to your right. The path climbs moderately to the right and becomes a pedestrian path (1.5, 580). It continues to climb and then levels out. Before you get to route 396 there are steps to climb. Climb over the security railing and take care as you cross the road. On the other side is a gate and a signpost pointing to Hadassah and Jerusalem (1.7, 600). The red-green markers of the Hadassah trail can sometimes be seen on signs placed in the ground.

Keep walking north on the dirt track as it curves east. Turn right at the fork, following the moderate upward gradient. A further gentle climb brings you to another fork (2.1, 610) where you will find a trail sign for those ascending to Ein Karem and for those descending to Ein Hindak, and a sign for the Hadassah trail. Keep going east at the fork. Hadassah medical center is now clearly visible above you. You will pass a picnic area, a high voltage pylon, and a Hadassah trail sign (point no. 13). Stop here to enjoy the magnificent vista (2.5, 600), then continue straight before turning right for a steep but short climb. Follow the path as it veers left between olive trees and Jerusalem pines. You will cross an avenue of cypresses. Between the trees on your right you can see a wooden sign indicating the entrance to the Hadassah trail (2.9, 635). Keep going east. A steep but very short climb on a concrete road leads to a dirt path. Continue east and arrive to the entrance way of the *Church of the Visitation* (3.3, 630). Turn right and after a short climb by steps arrive at the gate of the Church. **You can start the day at this point as indicated above**.

Luke 1:39-40: "Now Mary arose in those days and went into the hill country with haste, to a city of Judah, and entered the house of Zacharias and greeted Elizabeth." This event is the "Visitation" commemorated by the present church, which is reputed to stand on the site where the event took place.

The Church of the Visitation incorporates a natural grotto that once contained a small spring. The grotto was a place of worship in the Byzantine period, and the Crusaders erected a large, two-stories church over it. The church collapsed after the Crusaders left. In 1679 the site was bought by the Franciscans. Two centuries later they received permission from the Ottoman authorities to restore the church. The lower section was restored in 1862 and the upper church was completed in 1955, according to plans drawn up by Antonio Barluzzi.

Luke 1:46-49: "My soul magnifies the Lord, and my spirit has rejoiced in God my Savior. For He has regarded the lowly state of His maidservant; For behold, henceforth all generations will call me blessed; For He who is mighty has done great things for me and holy is His name".

One wall of the church courtyard is covered with ceramic tiles bearing the words of the Magnificat in more than 40 languages. Open: Apr.-Sept. 08:00-12:00; 14:30-18:00; Oct.-Mar. 08:00-12:00; 14:30:17:00. Gates are closed on Saturdays. Ring the bell to be admitted.

Return to the trail after the visit. Passing the boundary wall of the convent of the Rosary Sisters (3.35, 640) you will have a nice view of Ein Kerem. At Mary's Well (3.5, 640) turn left onto Hama'ayan Street and left again on Ein Kerem Street (3.8, 635), climbing gradually until you reach Kastel Square (4.0, 650). A blue and gold marker can be seen on the wall on the left side of Ein Kerem Street, opposite the parking lot.

Cross to the other side of Ein Kerem Street, go up Hatzelafim Street (medium gradient), and pass the Church of St. John the Baptist. Keep going east on Shvil Hatzukim Street until you come to a dirt road (4.8, 670) where you will see another blue marker. Keep going west, climbing gradually. Pass an entrance (5.1, 680) and continue east on the Shvil Hatzukim dirt road. The path veers to the left and climbs steeply through a grove. Go up the wooden stairs until you reach Hazikaron Street, the road leading left and west towards **Yad Vashem Holocaust Memorial Center. Open: Sun-Wed 09:00-17:00; Thu: 09:00-20:00; Fri: 09:00-14:00. Sat and holidays closed. Last entry is admitted one hour before the museum closes. Free**. Turn right and east and arrive at Holland Square and Herzl avenue (6.3, 820). Water and toilets are available at the entrance to Mt. Herzl. Turn left on Herzl Street and walk down the road to Bet Yad Sarah. Keep going straight and note the trail markers on the fence outside buildings 109 and 118. When you reach Kikar Denya (Denmark Square) (8.1, 760) turn right and cross Herzl Boulevard in the direction of Ariel Tamas Street (you will see a marker on the steps). After passing the monument to the fallen fighters of the Bet Hakerem neighborhood you will come to Hechalutz Street. Turn right at the Bet Hakerem council building and after 20 meters turn left into Haviva Reich Street. Continue straight on Hagai Street until you come to a public park (9.1, 760). Go through the park and walk across the pedestrian bridge straddling the Begin Expressway. Turn left at the end of the bridge, pass the Jerusalem Academy High School for Music and Dance and continue in the direction of the Givat Ram parking lot (toilets are available). Turn right and immediately left to the exit road from Givat Ram.

You will now come to Kaplan Street, opposite the Bank of Israel and Kiryat Hamemshala (the government complex) (9.7, 780). Turn right and continue on Ruppin Street until you reach the *Israel Museum intersection (9.5, 770). The museum is open: Sun, Mon, Wed, Thu, Sat 10:00-17:00; Tue 16:00-21:00; Fri: 10:00-14:00.* Turn left on Kaplan Street, go up to the Knesset area, and turn right at the first intersection. Follow the path as it curves left into the Rose Garden (9.9, 790). Take the time to visit the Menora located 50 meters above the road. From this vantage point you have an excellent view of the Knesset. (Some 20 meters further there are public facilities). Go back to the entrance of the Rose Garden, climb the steps and turn right on the asphalt path winding to the left. From this vantage point you can see both the Knesset and the Supreme Court. The layout is no accident, it was deliberately planned to symbolize the close connection between parliament and the court of justice. Keep going in the direction of the Supreme Court and then turn right and go back in the direction of the Knesset (toilets are available on your left, next to the fence of the Supreme Court). After descending approximately 100 meters turn right. The Knesset guards' station is located some 50 meters further (10.3, 800). Turn left and walk downhill in the direction of the bird watching station of the Society for the Protection of Nature in Israel. Here you will find a bird feeding station where wintering birds are ringed.

Continue walking down the hill, turn left in the direction of Sacher Park, and then right. Keep going straight until you reach the tunnel under Ruppin Street (11.0, 775). Cross at the tunnel and continue and turning left at another tunnel beneath Haim Hazaz Street (11.2, 770).

The Valley of the Cross is on your right. Continue straight down, turn right and you will arrive at the monastery. The Monastery of the Cross is a Byzantine structure. It derives its name from the tradition that the olive tree used to make Christ's cross grew at this site. The monastery was built in the 11th century over the remains of a 4th century monastery. Mon-Sat: 10:00-17:00 (fee).

Go back to the tunnel cross it and at the exit turn right to the sidewalk and after 20 meters turn sharply right. Another 200 meters will bring you to a beautiful view of the Valley of the Cross on your right. Now go up to your right until you reach Sa'adia Gaon Street and at the intersection with Metudela Street continue left on Sa'adia Gaon Street. The street name changes to Alfasi Street. Look for building no. 25. Prime Minister Menachem Begin and his wife Aliza lived here in the 1940s, in the basement apartment with green shades which is at the bottom of the path leading to the house. Continue on Alfasi Street. Some 100 meters further you will see on your left the tomb of Jason, a High Priest in the time of the Second Temple, during the Hellenist (Greek) period (12.3, 800). Turn right and continue on Radak Street, cross Aza Street and keep walking until you reach a parking lot, then turn right and walk up the road to the President's Residence (13.0, 800). Turn left at Shneourson square and after 100 meters turn left again onto Chopin Street.

On your right on Palmach Street is the Islamic Art museum, where you will find the famous David Lionel Salomons collection of Breguet watches. The pride of the collection is the watch designed for Marie Antoinette, who commissioned a timepiece that would incorporate every watch function known at that time. She never lived to see the watch, as it was only completed 34 years after her execution. In 1983 the famous watch collection was stolen by Na'aman Diller. After his death, some 25 years later, the watches were found and restored to the museum. The museum is open on Sun, Mon, Wed. 10:00-15:00; Tue, Thu 10:00-19:00; Fri 10:00-14:00 Sat 10:00-16:00. http://www.islamicart.co.il/en/

Continue Passing the Jerusalem Theater and continuing straight to Dubnow Street. When you come to a grove of pines – Gan Lior – continue to your right (there are no markers) onto a dirt path. Follow the path as it descends to Gedalia Alon Street, near the Hartman Institute. Turn left and continue to Dor

Vedorshav Street, where you will see a brown sign indicating that you have reached the Nature Museum. Water and toilets are available there.

Continue to Graetz Street (14.1, 760) and turn right. Turn left at Emek Refaim Street. Keep walking until you reach Mendes France Square (14.7, 760) by the gas station (water and toilets). Cross at the intersection and arrive at the gate of the Scottish Church and Hotel.

Day 9: Emek Refaim Street to the Holy Sepulchre - 6 km

Maps: 9-10. You can buy water along the trail.

Start at the gate of the Scottish Church Hotel (0.0, 760). Go down S.A. Nachon Street, pass by the **Menahem Begin Heritage Center**. *Open Sun, Mon, Wed, Thu 09:00-16:30; Tue: 09:00-19:00; Fri 09:00-12:30; Sat: Closed.* Continue down and cross the B'nai B'rith Bridge that spans Hebron Road (0.5, 740).

Bethlehem and the Church of the Nativity is just 8 kilometers to the south. To get to Bethlehem turn right and go up Hebron Road. Continue south and after about 4.5 kilometers you will cross the border to the Palestinian Authority. After 3.5 km you will arrive at Bethlehem. Check visa requirements at your consulate, a travel agency, or your hotel.

To visit the **Room of the Last Supper** do not turn right on the blue trail but continue down Hebron Road. Cross the bridge and turn right at the stop light (0.75, 730) on Hativat Yerushalaim Street. Turn left at a small parking lot (1.0, 750) and after 50 meters turn right into a narrow alley. Turn left through a gate (1.2, 760) to the traditional site of King's David Tomb. The Room of the Last Supper is located above King David's Tomb. Exit to an alley and you will see a set of stairs leading to the Room of the Last Supper (1.35, 760)

Mark 14:15-17 "And he will show you a large upper room furnished and ready; there prepare for us." And the disciples set out and went to the city and found it just as he had told them, and they prepared the Passover. And when it was evening, he came with the twelve". Open: Sat-Thu 08:00-17:00; Fri 08:00-13:00; Sun: Closed, free. Allow 15 minutes.

Opposite the Room of the Last Supper is **The Dormition of the Virgin Mary Abbey - Hagia Maria Sion**. *It was on this spot, near the Room of the Last Supper, that Mary died. The Basilica was built over the remains of a Byzantine church and was dedicated in 1910.* Open: Mon, Tue, Wed, Fri 8:30-12:00 and 12:30-18:00; Thu. 9:45-12:00 and 12:30-17:30; Sat. 8:30-12:00 and 12:30-17:30; Sun 10:30-11:45 and 12:30-17:30. Allow 30 minutes.

Retrace your steps through King David's Tomb and when you arrive back to the parking lot (1.7, 750) cross the street, turn right and go down. After a very short distance turn left and go toward Gey Ben Hinnom Street. At Ben Hinnom Street turn left and after another 300 meters you will have rejoined the trail (2.4, 700). The road drops at a steep gradient to the village of Silwan (2.6, 680). Turn left at the brown sign that points the way to Ir David (David's City). Continue another 300 meters along Hashiloach Street and after the road turns left (3.5, 685) a steep climb (to the left) will bring you to Ir David. If you want to continue on to the Old City and the Kotel you should turn left at the rise.

Walk through the village along Hashiloach Street until the paved road turns into a dirt road (3.9, 690). Markers can be seen on the electricity poles. The road climbs moderately until you enter the area of Har Hazeitim (Mt. of Olives) cemetery. The walls of the Old City tower over you on your left. Turn right, and you will see the grave of Zekharya ben Yehoyada, with the grave of Absalom immediately beyond (4.2, 700). Climb the steps towards Jericho Road. There are public toilets on the way. When you reach Jericho Road (4.4, 720) the Russian Church of Mary Magdalene with its gleaming golden onion-shaped domes will be on your right while the Old City is on your left. Turn left on Jericho road and follow the path in front of the Church of all Nations which stands next to the garden of Gethsemane (4.5, 730).

Matthew 26:36: Then Jesus went with his disciples to a place called **Gethsemane**, *and he said to them, "Sit here while I go over there and pray."*

To enter **Gethsemane** turn right on El-Manssuria Street. After a very short ascent turn right (4.7, 735). Ancient olive trees grow in the garden. The Church of All Nations stands on the remains of a Byzantine church that was destroyed by an earthquake in the 8th century, and a 12th century Crusader church which was abandoned in the 14th century. Open daily Oct-Mar: 08:00-12:00 and 14:00-17:00; Apr-Sep: 08:00-12:00 and 14:00-18:00.

Dominus Flevit Church is a small Franciscan church located on the upper western slope of the Mount of Olives. *According to Luke 19:41, "As he approached Jerusalem and saw the city, he wept over it" because "the days will come upon you when your enemies will...dash you to the ground."* According to tradition this was fulfilled in 70 CE, when the Romans destroyed Jerusalem. Dominus Flevit Church is believed to mark the place where Jesus' mourning over Jerusalem occurred. The current Dominus Flevit Church was commissioned by the Franciscans. It was designed by the Italian architect Anton Barluzzi. Constructed in 1954, the church is in the shape of a tear drop to symbolize the Lord's tears. The current church stands on the ruins of a 7th-century church, some mosaics of which still remain. The western window in Dominus Flevit provides a magnificent view of the Temple Mount. During the construction of the modern church, an ancient Jewish tomb dating to as early as the first century BC was discovered beneath. The tomb and several ossuaries (bone boxes) can be seen by visitors. The church is located on Mt. Olives few hundred meters above the Church of all Nations and Gethsemane. From Gethsemane turn right and an immediate right turn follows over a moderate ascent. Open: Daily 08:00-12:00; 14:30-17:00.

The Jerusalem trail goes right and up when you Leave Gethsemane. You turn left and down (there are public restrooms across the street, small fee). Turn right on Jericho road off the Jerusalem trail (there are no trail markers from this point) and go down to the **Tomb of the Virgin Mary**. Steps from the road descend into a square courtyard containing the upper church, which is a Crusader church with a vault for the family of King Baldwin the 2nd. The lower church at the bottom of the stairs is a Byzantine (5th century) **crypt**. There is an apse to the west and a longer, rock-cut apse to the east, in which **Mary's tomb** is marked by a small square chapel. Open daily: Mon-Sat 08:00-12:00 and 14:00-17:00.

Return to Jericho Road, turn right, make an immediate left turn and after a short climb you will come to the entrance to the Old City at the Lion's Gate (5.2, 760). Enter the Old City. For many Christian pilgrims to Jerusalem, their most important and meaningful experience is the walk along the **Via Dolorosa**, following the route taken by Jesus after his condemnation by Pilate, on his way to his crucifixion and burial. The Via Dolorosa has evolved since the 4th century un early Christianity, but for most pilgrims, the exact location of each event along the Via Dolorosa is of minor importance; the significance of the pilgrimage lies in its proximity to the original events and the opportunity to reflect upon them along the way. Stations are marked with a small plaque and are not easy to spot.

Below is a list of the stations along the Via Dolorosa:

Station 1: Where Jesus was condemned by Pontius Pilate. Today it is **the School of Madrasa al-Omariya,** 300m west of the Lion's Gate Open: Mon-Thu, Sat, 14:30-18:00; Fri 14:30-16:00.

Station 2: Where Jesus took up his cross. It is across the road from the first Station, in the Franciscan Monastery of the Flagellation,

Station 3: Where Jesus fell for the first time under the weight of his cross. It is marked by a relief sculpture above the door of a small Polish chapel at the junction with al-Wad Road.

Station 4: Where Mary watched her son pass by bearing the cross. It is commemorated at the Armenian Church of Our Lady of the Spasm. Inside the church is a Byzantine floor mosaic.

Station 5: Where Simon of Cyrene was forced by Roman soldiers to help Jesus carry the cross. It is located on the corner where the Via Dolorosa turns west off al-Wad Road and begins to narrow as it goes uphill.

Station 6 is commemorated by the **Greek Catholic Church of the Holy Face**.

Station 7: Where Jesus fell for a second time. It is marked by a Franciscan chapel at the junction of the Via Dolorosa and Souq Khan al-Zeit.

Station 8: Where Jesus consoled the lamenting women of Jerusalem. It is across the market street and up the steps of Aqabat al-Khanqah, opposite the Station VIII Souvenir Bazaar. A cross and the Greek inscription NIKA can be seen on the wall of the Greek Orthodox **Monastery of St. Charalambos.**

Station 9 is at the Coptic Patriarchate next to the Church of the Holy Sepulchre. Here, a Roman pillar marks the site of Jesus' third fall.

The remaining stations are inside The Church of the Holy Sepulchre (5.7, 800).

Station 10: Jesus is stripped - top of the stairs to the right outside the entrance.

Station 11: Jesus is nailed to the Cross, upstairs inside the entrance, at the Latin Calvary.

Station 12: Jesus dies on the Cross. Rock of Golgotha in the Greek Orthodox Calvary.

Station 13: Jesus is taken down from the Cross. Statue of Our Lady of the Sorrows – Latin Calvary.

Station 14: Jesus is laid in the Tomb, is inside the tiny chapel of the Holy Sepulchre.

The Church of the Holy Sepulchre, (6.0, 760) known as the Church of the Resurrection (*Anastasis*) to Eastern Orthodox Christians, is the holiest Christian site in the world. It stands on a site that is believed to encompass both Golgotha, or Calvary, where Jesus was crucified, and the tomb (Sepulchre) where he was buried. The Church of the Holy Sepulchre has been an important destination for pilgrims since the 4th century. The construction of the Holy Sepulchre was begun in 324 CE, under Emperor **Constantine the Great,** who converted to Christianity. It was destroyed by fire in 614 CE and rebuilt in 630 CE. Following a period of Moslem rule Emperor **Constantine Monomachos** provided money for its reconstruction in 1048. In later centuries it was damaged, and the Franciscans undertook its restoration in 1550. The structure was severely damaged by a fire in 1808 and an earthquake in 1927. Only in 1960 did major communities agreed on a plan of renovation. Open daily: Apr-Sep 05:00-20:00; Oct-Mar: 05:00-19:00.

Major sites in the Old City

The Western Wall and Temple Mount are within a short walking distance of the Church of the Holy Sepulchre.

The Western Wall - (The Kotel) : Open 24 hours. Make sure to visit the Western Wall tunnels. Open: Sun-Thu 07:00-18:00. Fri: 07:00-12:00. Guided tours only in Hebrew, English and French. (Fee).

Temple Mount: The Dome of the Rock and Al-Aksa Mosque. Summer: Mon-Thu 07:30-10:30; 13:30-14:30. Winter: Mon-Thu 07:30-10:30; 12:30-13:30. The mosques are closed to tourists.

Accommodations

Accommodations are listed from Nazareth to the Sea of Galilee and in Jerusalem. In Jerusalem there are numerous other options. The following accommodations are listed below: Trail angels, private and free camping sites, hostels and other budget accommodation, B&B and hotels. Contact information is provided for all types of accommodation where available. Many places have free internet access. Inquire upon reservation.

Trail angels and low-cost accommodations

There are a few trail angels along the trail. The list of trail angels is continuously updated on the web. The list also includes low cost accommodations along the trail. Trail angels are listed from north to south. Go to:

http://shvil.wikia.com/wiki/INT_Trail_Angels

Camping

Day 2: Lavi forest camping, free. Water and picnic tables. Restrooms are open 07:00-16:00. Located east of the Golani junction. From the gas station (day 2 km 12.0) do not cross route 77 but hike east on a dirt road and after approximately 500 meters you will arrive at a road that leads right and south to the camping site.

Sea of Galilee camping

Camping sites on the shores of the Sea of Galilee can be very crowded in spring and summer, especially on weekends and holidays.

Tamar beach camping. NIS 45. Shower, restrooms, restaurant. Cabins are available. Hike north from Migdal along route 90 for about 400 meters. Turn right on a road that arrives at the camp site after another 600 meters. Tel: 04-6790630;

Karei Deshe IYHA hostel is located at the Hukok beach. *An 8th century palace and a mosaic were found at nearby Hirbat Manim*. Tel: 1-599-510-511; e-mail: kdeshe@iyha.org.il.

Hostels and Inns

Sleep in dormitories or private rooms where available. Low rate indicates dormitories single occupancy, high rate is for private room double occupancy unless otherwise specified.

ILH - Israel Hostels: Nazareth, Tiberias, Kfar Tavor, Haifa, Tel-Aviv and Jerusalem and Odem on the Golan heights are the ILH hostels close to the trail and in major cities. ILH offers a wide choice of accommodations at competitive prices. Book on-line at: *www.hostels-israel.com*

Israel Youth Hostels Association (IYHA): Reservations are recommended. National reservation line: Tel: 1-599-510-511 press 4 for English, or book on-line at: *http://www.iyha.org.il/eng* . Poriya & Karei Deshe (near the Sea of Galilee – Kinneret – area), Tel Aviv, Jaffa and Jerusalem are the IYHA hostels closest to the trail or in major cities.

Nazareth

- *Fauzi-Azar Inn.* NIS 100 dormitories / NIS 440-500 double in a private room. Rates include breakfast. Located in the heart of Nazareth, just 5-minute walk from the Church of the Annunciation. Tel: 04-6020469; 054-4322328; *www.fauziazarinn.com*
- *Rosary Sisters Guest House.* Directions on their web site: http://www.rsisters.com/. Cell: 054-5533861.
- *Al-Mutran Guest House*: NIS 500 double. *www.al-mutran.com* Tel: 04-6457947; 052-7229090.
- *Sisters of Nazareth – Convent.* NIS 70 / 175-275. Tel: 04-6554304.
- *St. Margaret Hostel – Convent.* NIS 140 / 425. Tel: 04-657-3507.

Cana

Cana Guest House. NIS 100 / 300. Tel: 04-6517186; 04-6412375; Fax: 04-6518013. *www.canaguesthouse.com* . Contact them for directions.

Arbel

Shavit Hostel. NIS 120, B&B also available. NIS 550-800 double in private room. Tel: 04-6794919. E-mail: sara52@012.net.il .

Ginosar

Karei Deshe: IYHA hostel – NIS 450 B&B double. Located on the northeastern shore of the Sea of Galilee: E-mail: kdeshe@iyha.org.il ; Tel: 1-599-510511; 02-5945632. For directions see Hukok Beach camping.

Tiberias

Tiberias youth hostel: NIS 80-90 / 375. Tel: 04-679-2611; Fax: 04-6792411; http://www.tiberiashostel.com
Aviv youth hostel: NIS 75 / 275-325. Tel: 04-6712272   http://ilh.hostels-israel.com/hotel-aviv/hostel

B&B and family stay

B&B rates range between NIS 450-700 for double occupancy. Range indicates price on weekdays - weekends or holidays. All prices are in NIS (New Israeli Shekels) unless otherwise specified, and they are subject to change. Inquire if discount for Jesus trail hikers is available.

Zippori

Zippori village cottages B&B. Tel: 04-6462647; 057-7829568; E-mail: mspilcer@012.net.il
Zippori B&B: Tel: 04-6453373; 050-3100343.

Illaniya

Yehoshua B&B. Up to 8 people. Tel.: 054-4545210. For pickup and drop-off inquire when contacting the owner. E-mail: yehoshua18@walla.com.
Illaniya B&B. Up to 8 people. Pickup and drop-off available. Tel: 054-3137772; 04-676-9878.

Kfar Zeitim and Arbel

Kfar Zeitim B&B. Up to 16 guests. Tel: 04-6796629; 052-3493546.

Arbel B&B. Up to 40 guests. E-mail: arbelit@gmail.com. Tel: 04-6794325; 050-5700708.

Migdal

Beit Yehudit: *B&B.* Tel: 04-6724302; Cell: 052-2665238; Cell: 052-5208935 Max. capacity 16.

Weizman: *B&B.* Max. capacity 40. A 15% discount is provided to guests presenting this guide at check-in. Cell: 054-8015881; 0542400031; E-mail: yasmin_104@walla.co.il ;

Zohari: *B&B.* Tel: 04-67222304; Cell: 050-5502150; 050-6675087. Max. capacity 16.

Tabgha

Mount of Beatitudes Hostel - Convent. $54 single B&B. Half / full board available. Send a fax for reservations. Tel: 04-672-6712; Fax: 04-6726735 E-mail: ospbeat@netvision.net.il ;

Vered Hagalil

B&B. NIS 550. Book on-line at: www.veredhagalil.com ; Tel: 04-6935785 ; Fax: 04-6934964 ; See advertisement.

Korazim

Beit Haerez B&B. www.bet-haerez.com/len/. Up to 25 guests. Tel: 04-6860990; 054-4000833.

Jerusalem

City of Jerusalem web site: *http://tour.jerusalem.muni.il/eng*

Ein Karem – the Rosary Sisters Guest House: NIS 300 (single room) – 800 (4 beds). In Ein Karem, on the trail next to the Church of the Visitation and the Music Center. www.rosary-einkarem.com. Tel: 02-6413755; Fax: 02-6419790.

Abraham Hostel: 67 Hanevi'im street, Tel: 02-6502200 E-mail: reservations@abrahamhostels.com; *www.abrahamhostels.com* .

Jerusalem Hostel: Tel: 02-6236102; Fax: 02-6236092; E-mail: reservation@jerusalem-hostel.com. www.jerusalem-hostel.com

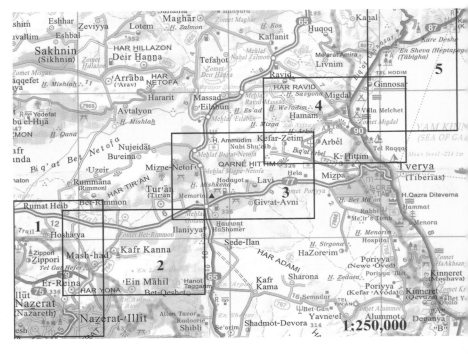

Basilica of the Annunciation

Nazareth

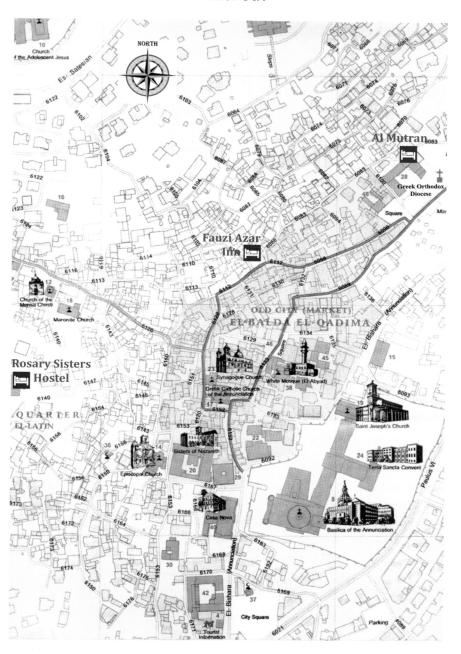

Legend scale: 1:50,000

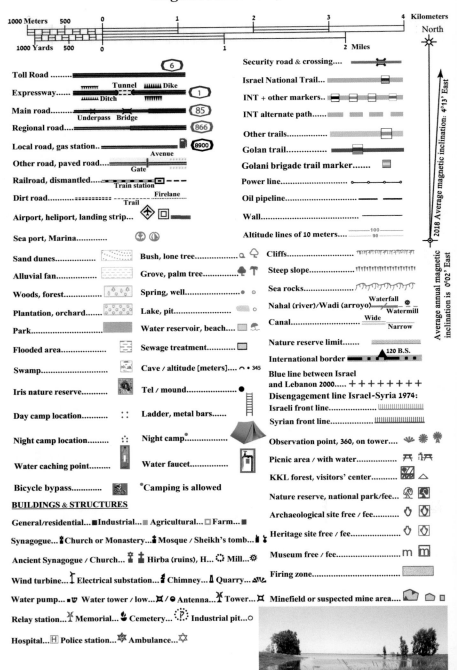

1000 Meters 500 — 0 1 2 3 4 **Kilometers**

1000 Yards 500 — 0 1 2 **Miles**

North

Toll Road 6

Tunnel   Dike

Expressway...... Ditch 1

Main road......... Underpass   Bridge 85

Regional road.... 866

Avenue

Local road, gas station.. 8900

Other road, paved road.... Gate

Railroad, dismantled.... Train station

Firelane

Dirt road......... Trail

Airport, heliport, landing strip...

Sea port, Marina.............

Sand dunes................

Alluvial fan................

Woods, forest...............

Plantation, orchard.......

Park.............................

Flooded area..............

Swamp........................

Iris nature reserve...........

Day camp location.........

Night camp location.........

Water caching point.........

Bicycle bypass.............

BUILDINGS & STRUCTURES

General/residential...■ Industrial...■ Agricultural...□ Farm...■

Synagogue...✿ Church or Monastery...✿ Mosque / Sheikh's tomb...✿ ✿

Ancient Synagogue / Church...✿ ✿ Hirba (ruins), H...✿ Mill...✿

Wind turbine...Ɪ Electrical substation...✿ Chimney...◖ Quarry...▲Ⱡ

Water pump...▪ⱱ Water tower / low...Ⱶ / ⊝ Antenna...Ⱦ Tower...Ⱶ

Relay station...Ⱦ Memorial...♣ Cemetery...∴ Industrial pit...○

Hospital...Ⱨ Police station...✿ Ambulance...✡

Bush, lone tree.................

Grove, palm tree.............

Spring, well.....................

Lake, pit.......................

Water reservoir, beach....

Sewage treatment.............

Cave / altitude [meters].... ⌒ • 345

Tel / mound..................●

Ladder, metal bars......

Night camp.*..................

Water faucet................

*Camping is allowed

Security road & crossing....

Israel National Trail...

INT + other markers..

INT alternate path......

Other trails.................

Golan trail.................

Golani brigade trail marker.......

Power line....................

Oil pipeline..................

Wall..............................

Altitude lines of 10 meters.... 100 / 90

Cliffs..............................

Steep slope...................

Sea rocks....................

Waterfall

Nahal (river)/Wadi (arroyo)... Watermill

Wide

Canal.............................. Narrow

Nature reserve limit.......

International border........ ▲ 120 B.S.

Blue line between Israel
and Lebanon 2000..... + + + + + + +

Disengagement line Israel-Syria 1974:

Israeli front line...................

Syrian front line.................

Observation point, 360, on tower....

Picnic area / with water.................

KKL forest, visitors' center...........

Nature reserve, national park/fee...

Archaeological site free / fee..........

Heritage site free / fee...................

Museum free / fee.......................... m

Firing zone..................

Minefield or suspected mine area....

2018 Average magnetic inclination: 4°13' East

Average annual magnetic inclination is 0°02' East

Basilica of the Annunciation

Mona Lisa of the Galilee in Tzipori

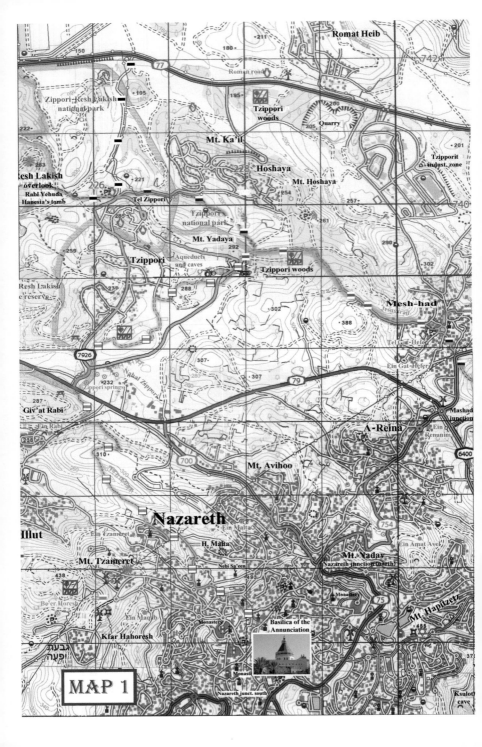

Valley of Tur'an

Moshav Arbel and the Arbel Valley. Mt. Arbel (right), Mt. Nitai (left) and the Sea of Galilee

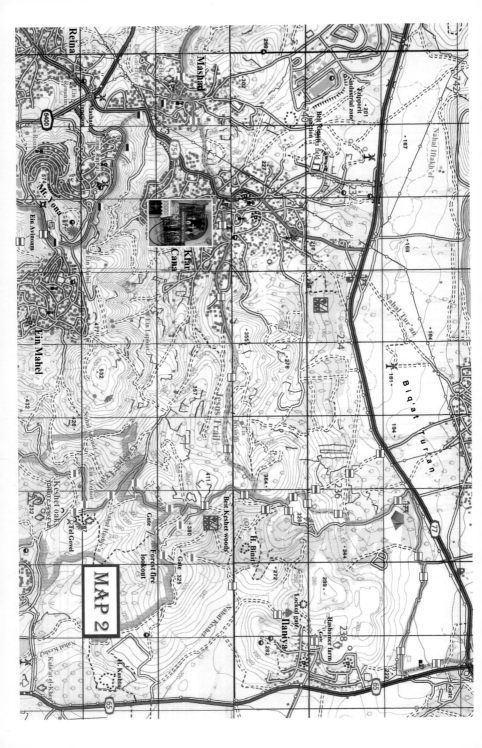

Nabi Shu'ayb

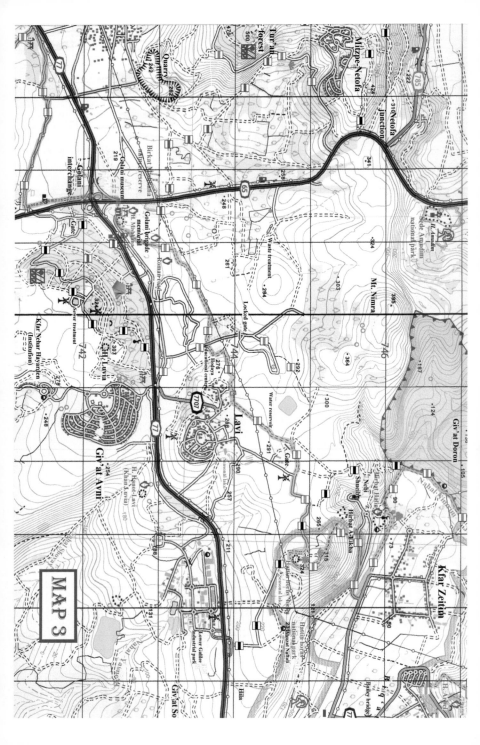

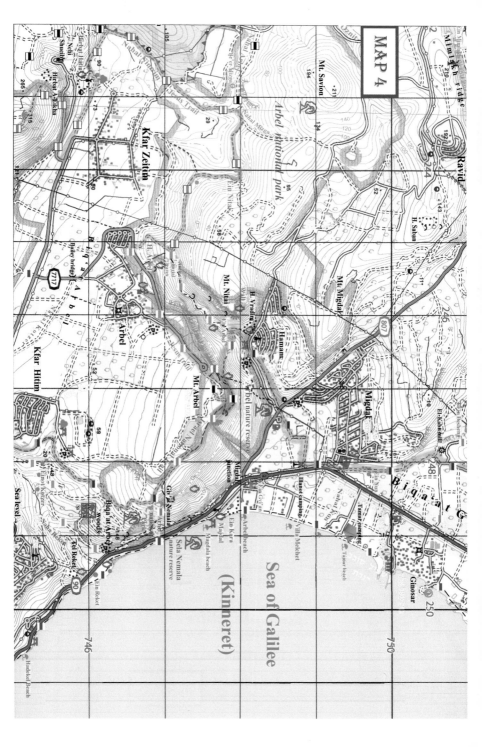

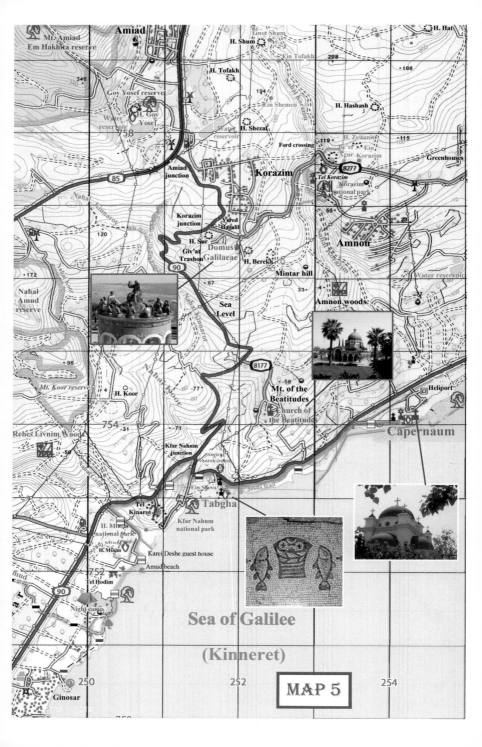

MAP 5

Tabgha, Mt. Arbel (left), Horns of Hattin (middle distance), Mt. Nitai (right)

Mosaic of Loaves and Fish in the Church of the Multiplication (left),
Fourth Century Synagogue, Capernaum

SURVEY OF ISRAEL

JERUSALEM

LEGEND

Built-up area, Public building ....

Public park or Woodland.........................

Synagogue ⚎ Church ⚏ Mosque ⚊

Main road, divided ....

Road, Tunnel, Bridge .... ─] ─ [─ ✕

Unpaved road, Fuel station...........

Promenade or Pedestrian Mall ...... ////////////////

Railway...............................

Motorway, Highway ....

Main street ....

Other street...........................

Interurban road numbers:

Motorway ①   Highway 60

Regional road 446   Local road 3985

Jerusalem trail

Scale

0	100	200	300	400	500	600	700	800	900	1000

Metres   Metres

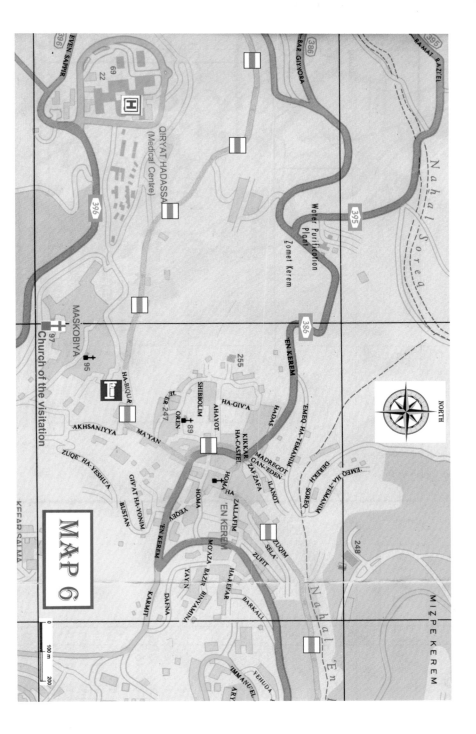

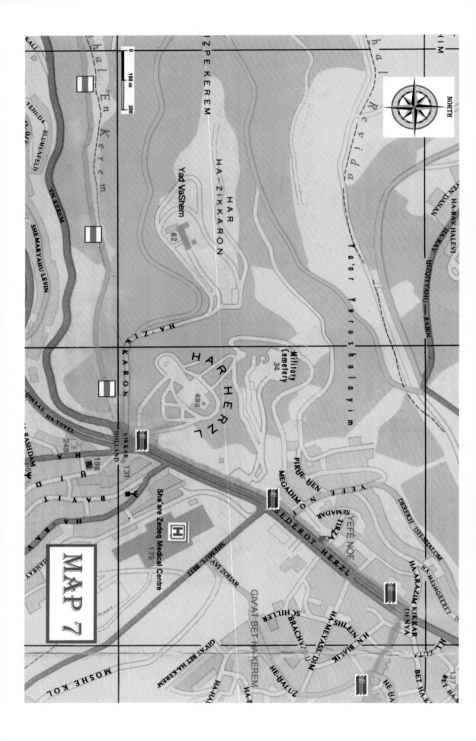

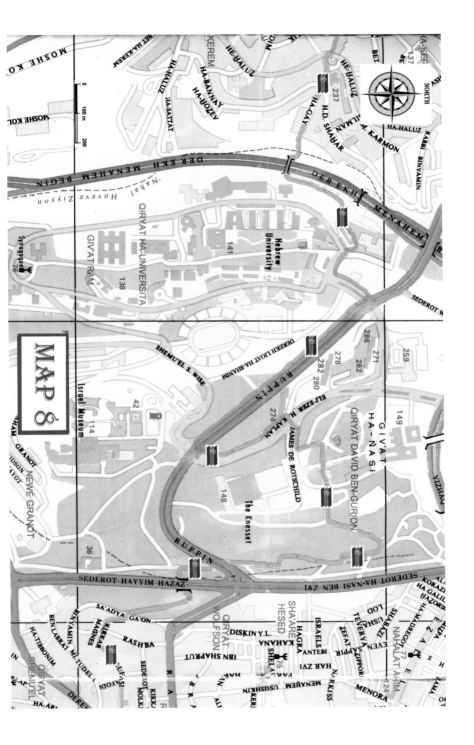

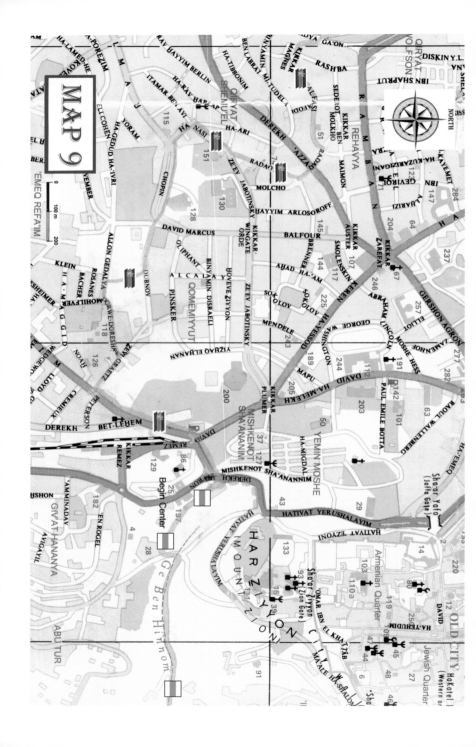

Room of the Last Supper

Russian Orthodox Church of Mary Magdalene on Mt. of Olives (left)
Hagia Maria Sion Abbey - Dormition of the Virgin Mary on Mt. Zion (right)

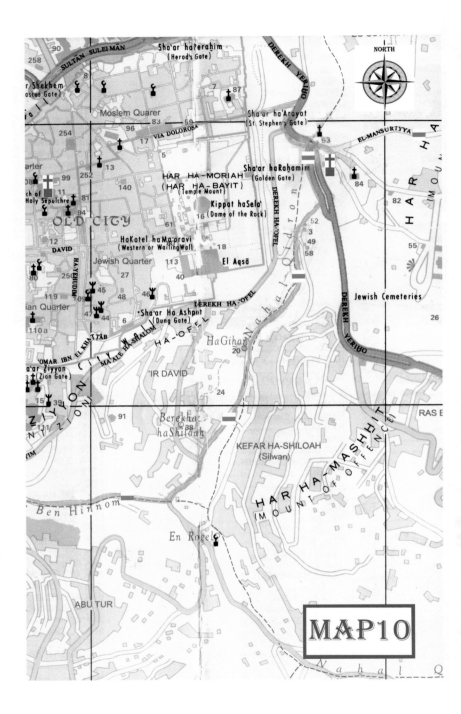

Dome of the Rock – View from Mt. of Olives

The Holy Sepulchre, Ninth Station (left)
The Tomb of Christ, Fourteenth Station (right)

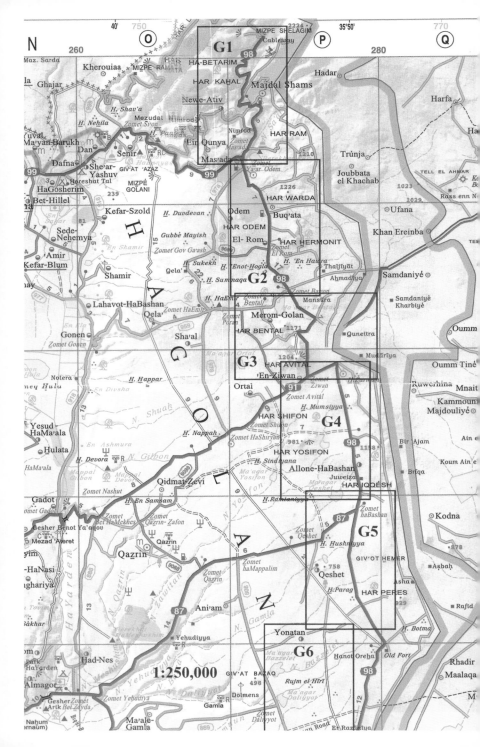

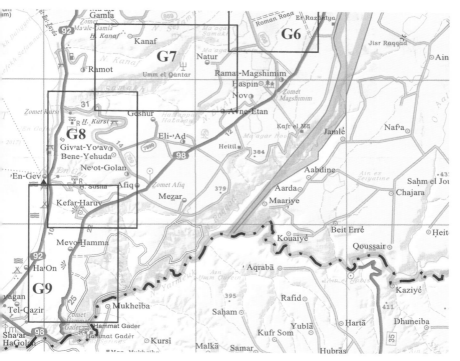

Golan Iris

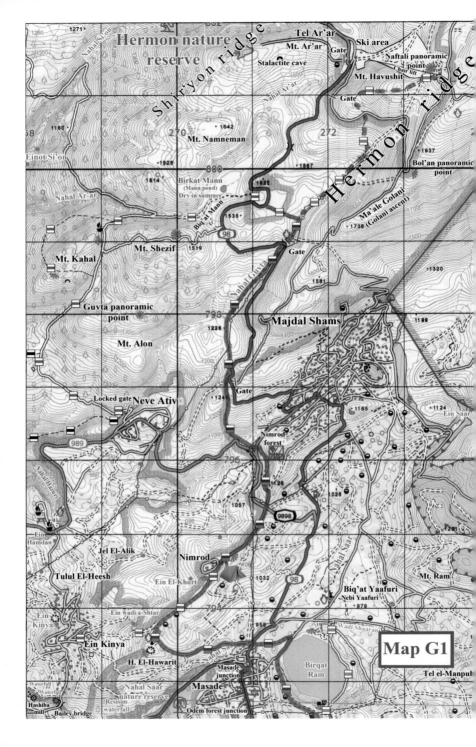

Chairlift to Mt. Havushit - misty morning

Hiking at 2000 meters - Mt. Havushit

Mesopotamian Iris on Mt. Hermon

Herd of wild boars on Mt. Hermon

Neve Ativ, Nimrod fort and Hula valley

Birqat Ram

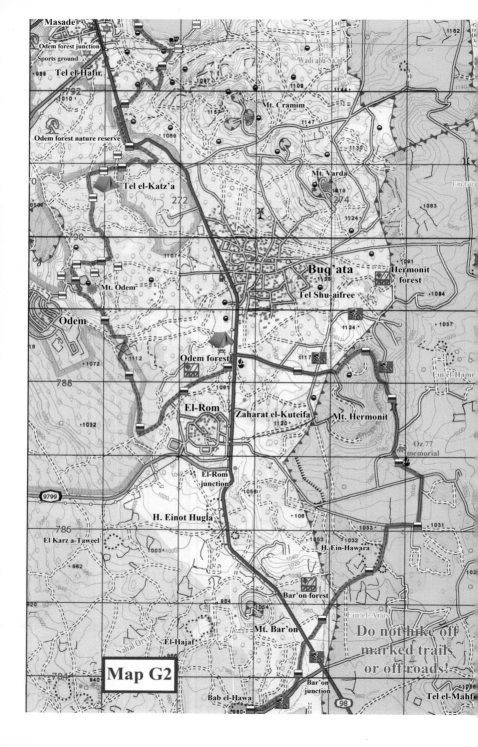

Cherry trees near Buqata

Scoria quarry on mount Odem

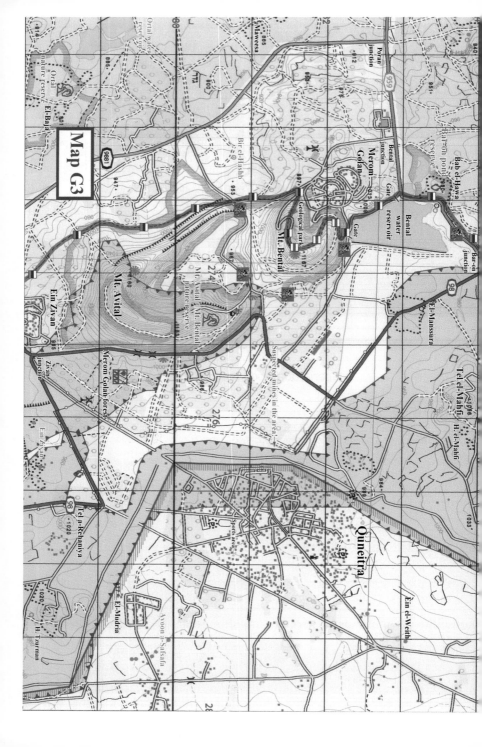

Map G3

Mount Bental

Wind turbines - Mount Bnei Rasan

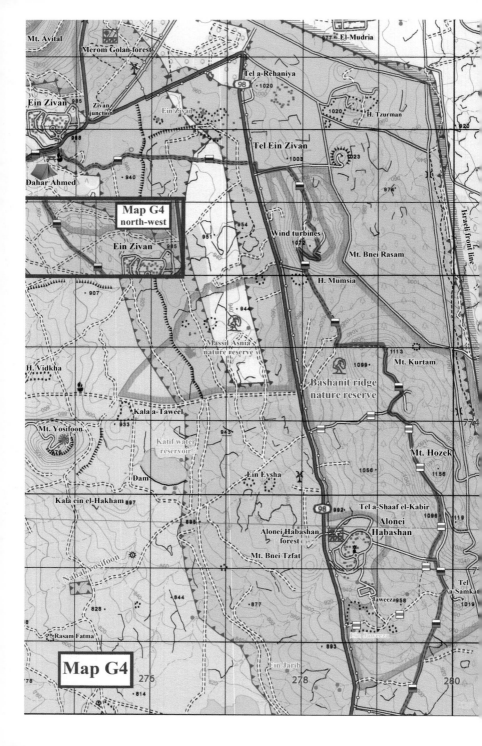

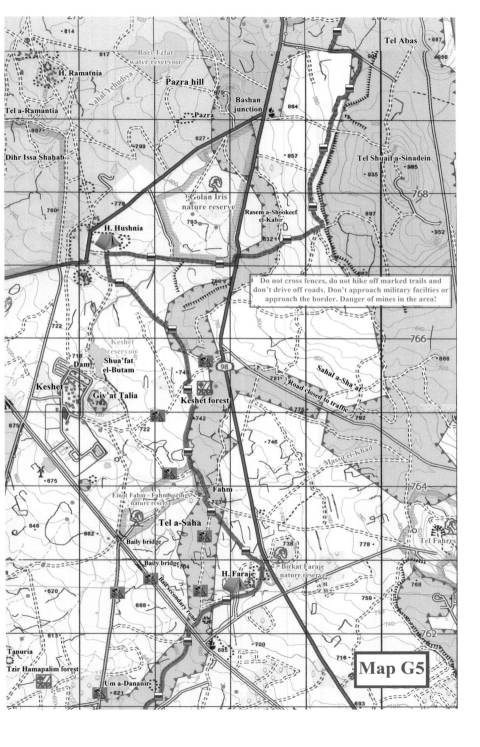

Do not cross fences, do not hike off marked trails and don't drive off roads. Don't approach military facilties or approach the border. Danger of mines in the area!

Map G5

Alonei Habashan - Bashan Oaks

Daliot reservoir

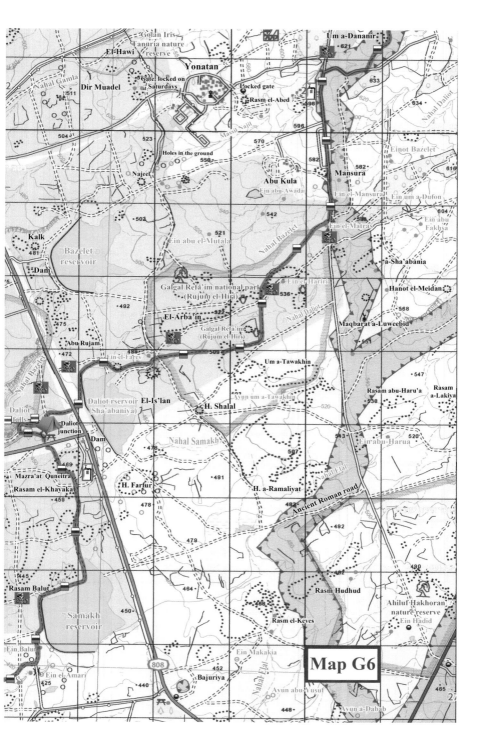

Map G6

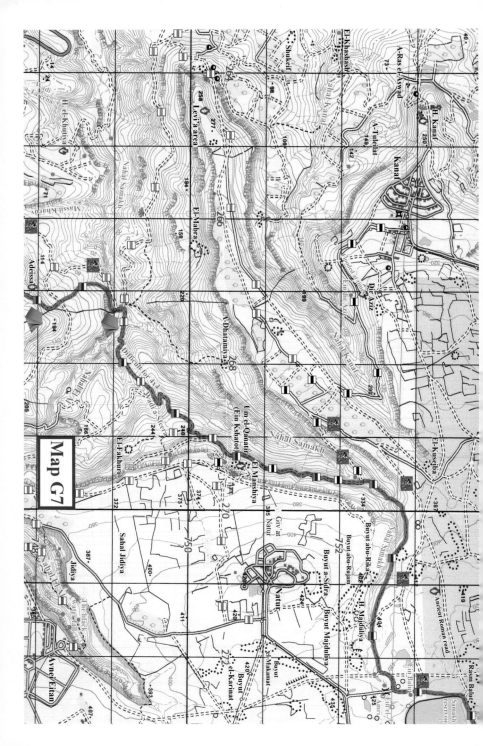

Map G7

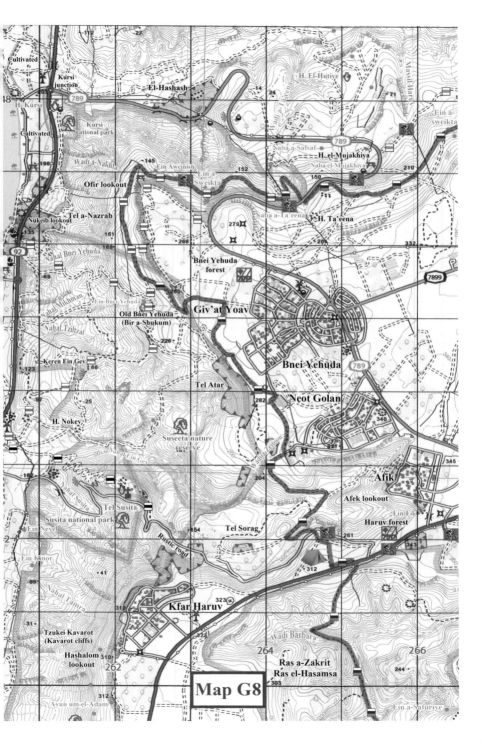

Map G8

Nahal Daliot

Synagogue in Um el-Qanatir

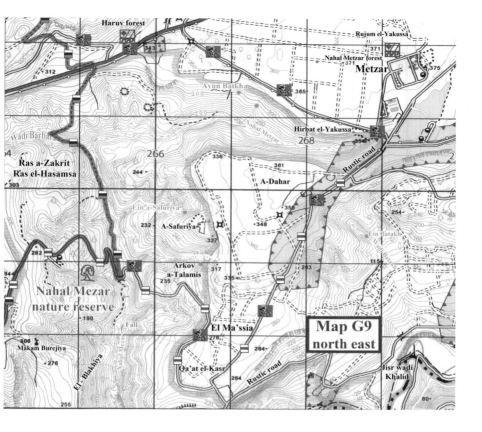

Sea of Galilee

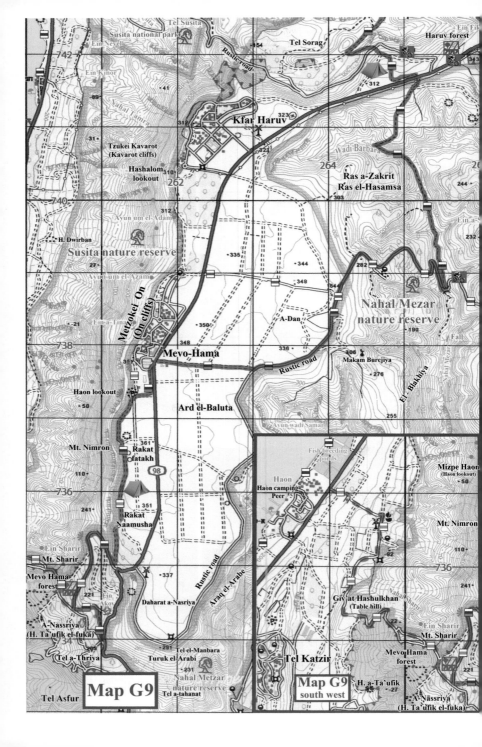

Jacob Saar   Yagil Henkin

The Golan Trail

Second Edition

Reviewed by Dany Gaspar

Table of Contents

Important information

Forum: https://www.tapatalk.com/groups/israeltrail/golan-trail-f40/

Your comments about the guide are always appreciated. Please post them on the forum and they will be available to all hikers. Thank you.

www.tapatalk.com/groups/israeltrail/your-comments-about-the-guide-t609.html

GPX file: Please send a private message on the forum to the administrator.

Geology, fauna, flora and population

The Golan Heights are part of the Bashan, a region situated mostly in Syria. The region's basalt plateau is one of the largest in the world. The volcanic activity in the Golan is geologically young, dating on its west side to the second millennium BCE. Apart from basalt, the plateau is covered with scoria and tuff. In the south, in areas that are not basaltic, sedimentary rocks from earlier periods such as limestone and chalk can be discerned.

As we know from the Old Testament, the Golan was once forested: "...Give cries of grief, O you oaks of Bashan, for strong trees of the world have come down". (Zechariah 11:2). Cutting down trees for construction, commerce, and heating critically damaged the forests of the plateau. Today only remnants of the magnificent forest can be seen. They are located in isolated forest reserves, the largest of which is the Odem forest, through which the trail passes. Aleppo oak and oak are commonly found here. The dominant vegetation is Mediterranean, and in springtime the flowering is spectacular. The magnificent Golan Iris is located next to the trail in the Hushniya region.

The fauna here is among the most diverse in the country. You will encounter large mammals, birds of prey, and fish in creeks. Vulture-watching is common, especially in nesting areas in and above streams. Wild boars, foxes, deer and jackals are frequently seen. It is rare to encounter wolves despite their extensive distribution; according to the Nature and Parks Authority, there are over 100 wolves in the Golan Heights in 15 packs. In the 80s' the deer population numbered several thousand, but their population has dwindled to only a few hundred because they have fallen prey to wolves. The local sheep and cattle population has also been affected, although efforts by the authorities have reduced the rate of predation by about half.

Evidence of human settlement has been discovered in the Golan from as far back as the prehistoric period, based on agriculture and grazing. Numerous archaeological findings suggest that the Golan Heights was inhabited from the Stone Age to the Byzantine period. The ancient Via Maris that linked Egypt to the ancient empires of Syria and Mesopotamia passed here, thus contributing to the settlement continuum. The Roman Empire built a network of roads, some of which you will pass or hike on your journey. There are many remains from the Byzantine period, most of them in the southern part of the plateau. A severe earthquake hit the area in 749 CE, destroying many settlements on the Golan Heights and the Sea of Galilee. During the Crusader period (1099-1291) knights passed here from

Syria to Jerusalem. The battle of the Horns of Hattin in 1187, in which Saladin defeated and destroyed the Crusader army under the command of Guy de Lisignan and Raymond III of Tripoli, marked the beginning of the end of the first "Kingdom of Jerusalem." On the Golan the Muslims built the mighty fortress of Nimrod which dominated the road to Damascus. During the Mamluk and Ottoman periods the Golan continued to be an important transit route, and settlements were built along its roads.

There was renewed Jewish settlement in the Golan at the end of the 19th century, when ultra-Orthodox residents of Safed purchased land in the center and south of the Golan Heights. They settled in Bnei Yehuda but their attempts failed and the site was abandoned. The remains of Bnei Yehuda are visible from the trail west of Giv'at Yoav. Following the defeat of the Ottoman Empire in the First World War the Middle East was divided between the victorious powers. The Golan was transferred to Syria and a French mandate was established. Syria gained independence in 1946 and continued to rule the Golan until the Six-Day War. During this period the communities of the Hula Valley suffered constant shelling from the Syrians. In June 1967 Israel seized control of the Golan, which had been abandoned by its inhabitants with the exception of four Druze villages in the north. Today the population of the Golan is close to 50,000, of whom about 50% are Druze, 48% are Jewish and 2% are Muslim Alawites. The economy relies on industry, agriculture and tourism. In some agricultural sectors the Golan provides for about one-third of Israel's consumption. The Golan Druze export apples to Syria.

The season to hike, hike direction and biking the trail

The best season to hike the Golan Trail is spring, which lasts longer here than in any other region in the country because of the relative height of the terrain. It's also pleasant to hike in the fall. In winter one has to wear warmer clothing. When it rains or snows it's difficult to hike and the trail becomes muddy. In the hot summer months, the hike is not pleasant but doable if you insist. You must rest in the shade during the hot hours of the day, and make sure to drink plenty of water.

The trail is ~125 km long and for an average hiker it takes 6-7 days to complete. We've chosen to divide the route into seven days, including the descent to the shore of the Sea of Galilee, which adds 7 km to the route. Hiking in the Golan does not require coordination with the army. The hike direction is north to south. Very few hikers choose to hike from south to north. The descent from Mount Hermon ends in a very steep section. Hikers who start the trail without proper physical preparation are at a higher risk of injury. The sun will be at your back if you hike from the south. By the time you reach Mt. Hermon you will be in better physical shape and it will be easier to climb the mountain. In spring high vegetation covers many trail markers. If you lose your way, go back to the last visible trail marker and resume your hike from there. In rainy years the trail may be "drowned" in water reservoirs, as occurred during the winters of 2010 and 2011 in the Samakh reservoir area. In such a case, the flooded section should be bypassed. There are explanatory signs in Hebrew every 7-10 km.

Biking the trail is possible, but some detours are required. They are clearly marked on the maps.

Getting to the trailhead, taxis and transportation back.

To reach the trailhead on Mt. Hermon: Take bus #58 from Kiryat Shmona to Majdal Shams. From there hitchhike or take a taxi. The gate at Majdal Shams opens at 08:00. You can also spend the night before the hike in Nimrod. Tawafiq, the second endpoint of the trail, is accessible only by hitchhiking. Those who finish or start in Ha'on should use Egged bus lines 966 (Jerusalem-Katzrin) and 843 (Tel Aviv-Katzrin), or line 51 (Tiberias-Hispin) of Golan-bus, or a combination of two lines via the Tzemach junction. Below are taxi telephone numbers on the Golan heights. Fixed price taxi rides are always more expensive than paying according to the meter.

Majdal Shams: Hassan Sabag – 050-5302866
Buq'ata: Ala – 052-4420275; Yusuf M'jad – 052-6999072
Yonatan: Hananiya Ben Tzvi – 052-8348361
Eliad: Dani Aviram – 052-2616637

Water, food, accommodations and trail angels.

Do not drink water from reservoirs and streams without boiling. Cattle herds are a source of pollution. Purification of water using filters or iodine is not sufficient and water should be boiled after purification. It is forbidden to wash or swim in water reservoirs. Water and food are available in villages and kibbutzim near the trail. Most have a mini-market or a grocery store. Please keep in mind that on Fridays they close early (14:00-15:00) and on Saturdays all are closed. In order to resupply you will need to hike off the trail.

There are no free official night camps on the Golan Trail. Camping is permitted for almost all its length, except in nature reserves. The maps are marked with

places suitable for setting up a tent. In some villages there are paid camping sites with showers and restrooms. Private camp sites and hostels are not free of charge. They are all listed together with the trail angels on the link below:
https://shvil.wikia.com/wiki/Golan_Trail

There are B&B and grocery stores in almost every village and kibbutz; information about **B&B** and **Airbnb** can be found on the internet.

Safety

Crossing grazing areas: Please cross grazing areas only at designated crossings, and close the gates behind you.

Hiking after sunset: Please plan to complete ther hike before sunset. If you are caught in the dark, stop and set up your tent wherever you are or call for help.

IDF permits: To hike the Golan trail, coordination with the IDF is not required. If you start the hike at the upper chairlift station on Mt. Havushit, you must call the IDF to coordinate: 04-6966207.

When camping out: In order to keep animals away - wild boars in particular – the food in your backpack should be properly wrapped, including leftovers.

Camp fire: Avoid camp fires and do not burn toilet paper. Sparks flying in the wind can start huge fires. This is especially important between late spring and early winter, when vegetation is dry. Please heat food under supervision only using a gas or alcohol stove. Toilet paper should be buried in the ground or else carried in a bag to the nearest trash can.

Minefields: There are numerous minefields on the Golan Heights. They are all behind fences and clearly marked. Do not stray from the trail and never cross the fences.

Mount Hermon

In order to start the Golan Trail [GT] hike on Mt. Hermon at 2,050 m, you should be in a reasonable physical shape. Spring is the best time for the GT hike, particularly from March to late May or mid-June. At 2,000 meters snow still covers the ground in March until late April. Check the snow conditions before taking the chairlift to the upper skiing station. If snow prevents safe hiking at 2,000 meters start the hike at the beginning of the GT.

To arrive to Mt. Hermon, take bus #58 from Kiryat Shmona to Majdal Shams. From Majdal Shams to Mt. Hermon hitchhike or take a taxi to the skiing area at 1600 m. From there take a chairlift (fee) to the upper skiing station at 2,050 meters. Taxi in Majdal Shams: 050-530-2866 Hassan. Taxi in Buq'ata 052-442-0275 Ala. **The gate on the road from Majdal Shams to Mt. Hermon opens at 08:00.**

We recommend spending the night before the hike in **Nimrod** at **Bekatot Ba'arafel** 04-6984218, 052-2697718, they have a camping area, dormitories and B&B. Alternatively stay at Ohel Avraham 052-2821141 in large tents. **Majdal Shams** B&B 050-7194982 or 04-6982844, and **Narkis hotel** 04-6982961 or Legacy Village hotel: 04-6870173 or 052-6251435. Camping out is not allowed on Mt. Hermon above Neve Ativ. Wild camping is allowed by Sheikh Ottman / Nebi Hazuri, or in Nimrod forest.

Day 1H: Start on Mt. Havushit - 4 km

Map: G1. Drinking water: 3 liters. Refill in Nimrod.

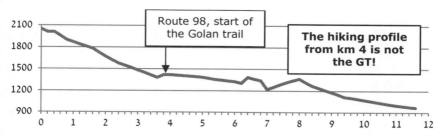

You have to contact the IDF at least two days in advance, and let them know that you plan to hike the green trail from Mt. Havushit at 2,000 meters. Contact tel.: 04-6966207. The IDF might decline your request. If this is the case, start the hike beginning of the GT, Day 1.

In late spring and particularly in June the National Parks Authority (NPA) closes for hiking all the area above 1,200 m. because of the nesting season. In winter when the ski area is open, there is an entry fee which is collected at the gate at km 4.0.

Start the day at the upper skiing station (0.0, 2,050). **When the Yom Kippur war started, the Israeli military outpost in the area was captured by the Syrian army on October 6th, 1973. Two weeks later, following a failed attempt, Israeli Golani brigade troops and paratroopers captured both the Israeli and the Syrian outposts.**

Exit the skiing station to the right and take the green trail down. Follow the green trail, take a left turn (0.2, 2010) and after a short distance turn right (0.35, 1990). **In May and June, you'll see the beautiful blossoms of various flowers typical of the area, particularly the Mountain Horned Poppy.** The trail goes in a rocky area. After a steep descent at (0.75, 1910) turn left and arrive to Ma'ale Golani road (1.6, 1780). It is named after the Golani brigade that fought here in 1973. Cross the road and continue the descent. **In May the Mesopotamian Iris is in full bloom. The Mesopotamian Iris (Hebrew: Iris Aram Nahara'im) is endemic to the northern parts of Israel, while in other places of the country it is found by old Muslim cemeteries where it was cultivated.**

At (2.0, 1670) the trail makes a left turn. *Watch the trail markers, it is easy to miss them here, particularly in Spring. Wild boars live in the area. When I last hiked here I (JS) met a large herd of about 30 adult and young boars at ~11 a.m. They are harmless but don't get too close to them. They might reconsider their attitude if feel threatened.* The trail turns right onto a dirt road (2.4, 1575). Continue a mild descent along a power line. Arrive at trails crossing with the Golan Trail (3.5, 1395). If you turn right and climb the dirt road you will arrive at the starting point of the Golan Trail (3.8, 1420). Continue straight and down on the GT. There is another marker on the powerline pole: Green/Yellow/Green. This is the **Golani Brigade trail marker**.

The Golani Brigade Trail is the initiative of Brigadier General (ret.) David Katz, who commanded the Brigade in the late 70's. The Golani was the first brigade of the IDF and therefore it is Brigade #1. The Golani trail winds among sites where the brigade has engaged in battles since 1948. It starts on Mt. Hermon, where the brigade fought in 1973 and ends in Eilat, where the brigade arrived in 1949 to establish the southernmost border of Israel. Umm Rashrash, as it was called, was a mandatory British police compound, located ~5 km off the northern shore of the Gulf of Eilat. The capture of Umm Rashrash at the conclusion of Operation Ovdah was the final stage of the War of Independence. Under Israeli rule the place developed into the city of Eilat. The hut that remained from the Umm Rashrash police station has been declared a heritage site. The Golani trail is the longest trail in Israel, some 1,200 km in length. About 20% of the Golani trail follows the same path as the Israel National Trail.

Day 1: From Mt. Hermon to Tel Katz'a - 13 km

Map: G1. Water 3-4 liters. Refill in Nimrod and in Mass'ade. If you camp out by Tel Katz'a buy sufficient food and water in Mass'ade.
Bikers will start the ride in Nimrod or use the road from Mt. Hermon to Nimrod.

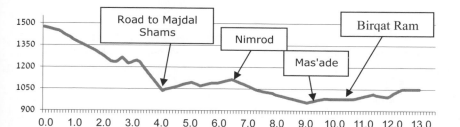

The descent to Majdal Shams is steep and rocky. Early morning fog can cause a problem at higher elevations, and sometimes it is dense. In winter snow might also be an issue at the beginning of the trail. Consider skipping the initial section if snow or dense fog cover the area.

Mt. Hermon is mentioned in Deuteronomy, chapter 3: "Thus, by then we had taken the country of the two Amorite kings beyond the Jordan, stretching from the Wadi Arnon to Mount Hermon. The Sidonians call Hermon 'Sirion' and the Amorites call it 'Senir." In chapter 4 Mt. Hermon is referred to as Mt. Sion: "From Aroer on the edge of the Arnon Valley, all the way to Mount Sion, that is, Hermon." Its Arabic name is Jebel a-Sheikh - the old mountain. The mountain is made of limestone dating from the Jurassic period. Flora and fauna on the mountain are characteristic of the area. The Syrian bear lived here until the beginning of the twentieth century. The last sighting was recorded in 1917, when the last bear was hunted in the Majdal Shams area. The peak of the Hermon, at an altitude of 2,814 m, is in Syria. Its highest point in Israel is 2,224 meters. During the Yom Kippur War in 1973 Mt. Hermon was captured by the Syrians and the soldiers stationed there were taken prisoner. The mountain was subsequently reoccupied by Israel. In response to a question posed by TV reporter Micha Limor, private Benny Massas of Battalion 51 of the Golani Brigade replied that they attacked the mountain because "we were told that the Hermon is the eyes of the country."

Start the day by the Hermon ticket box (0.0, 1475) turn right and east, and cross the parking lot. At the east end of the parking lot you will find the Golan Trail mark and explanatory notes (in Hebrew) on a large sign of the trail (0.2, 1485). Go down on a dirt road marked green. At a fork (0.5, 1450), the green path continues to the left to the top of Mt. Hermon. The Golan Trail turns right and goes down along a power line. **On the right side and well above the trail there are remains of the ancient settlement of Bir A-Zuba.**

Cross route 98 (0.9, 1405) Turn right and after a few meters turn left again onto a dirt road in Nahal Guvta and continue along the power line. Passing some boulders, the GT turns slightly left, and leaves the Guvta creek; Pass by a small grove (2.5, 1235). Leave the power line and climb on moderate rocky ascent. Cross the remains of a fence (2.7, 1265) and continue on a moderate descent alongside the fence. Turn left (2.9, 1225) and follow a moderate ascent on a dirt road (3.1, 1240). Cross a cattle grid, leave the dirt road and climb few rocks with pegs. At the top of the ascent Birqat Ram is visible to the south. Start a very steep and rocky descent (3.3, 1235). Take some extra caution here. At the Neve Ativ-Majdal Shams road (3.9, 1025) turn left. At a T junction (4.2, 1045) turn left and after 200 meters turn right and climb the trail to Nimrod forest (4.5, 1060). **The name Majdal Shams means "tower of the sun". It is the highest village in the country, some 1170 meters above sea level. As of 2017, it had 11,000 residents, whose livelihood is mainly based on agriculture and tourism.**

Continue on a mild ascent in the Nimrod forest and turn left (4.8, 1080). Arrive at a dirt roads crossing (5.1 1095). Turn right and pass by Nimrod junction (5.4, 1070). Continue straight on the road passing by orchards. Pass by Ohel Avraham campground (6.3, 1105) on your right. Arrive at the entrance to Nimrod (6.5, 1115). On the left is a great view of Birqat Ram and the village of Mass'ade. **Nimrod was established in 1982 as a pseudo-military settlement. In 1999 it became a civil settlement. Its name comes from the Nimrod Fortress, located to the northwest on the western slopes of Mt. Hermon.**

Before Nimrod's gate turn left on a dirt road marked in red. Go down the dirt road. If you check the view on your right you will see **Ein Qinya, a picturesque Druze village.** At a T junction the red trail turns right and goes down to Ein Kinya. We turn left towards the village of Mas'ade (7.7, 1030). Pass on your right by Nebi Elya locality (7.9, 1020). Nebi Elya, named after the prophet Elijah, is usually closed to visitors.

Cross the Saar creek. **In winter and early spring, the flow of water can be strong. A few mills were located along the stream near Majdal Shams and**

in the lower part near Ein Qinya. Arrive in the village of Mas'ade on route 98 (9.2, 960). **In 2017 there were 3,500 residents here.** Cross route 98 and continue straight. The road turns into a dirt road, ending at a T junction. Turn right (9.9, 980). We hike now above Birqat Ram. **Birqat Ram is the result of a volcanic eruption. Its' water is used for irrigation, and the maximum depth is about 10 meters. In 1985 Prof. Naama Goren-Inbar discovered a small female icon at the bottom of Birqat Ram, estimated to be about 250,000 years old. This figurine is considered to be the oldest human-shaped archaeological artifact in the world.**

Continue on the road, which curbs and climbs near a pumping station on a moderate ascent (10.7, 980). A green trail goes left next to a power line, and we turn right onto a paved road (11.4, 1015). Continue on a dirt road near a pumping station (11.7, 1000). At a fork turn right, reach T junction and turn left onto a dirt road with green markers (11.9, 995). Arrive at route 98 (12.4, 1050), cross it and turn left. **Bikers** will continue on a paved road for a detour of Tel Katz'a on its' western side. Cross a red trail and continue straight uphill. **You hike an ancient Roman road made of basalt stones** (13.0, 1050) at the foot of Tel Katza, this is where the day ends.

Wild camping is allowed in the area. You can stay in private camp grounds in Nimrod, in Elrom or by Birqat Ram. In Odem there is a hostel. You can hike to Odem on the red trail, it's ~2 km. Airbnb is available in the area, check the web. All places can be reached in 5-10 minutes by taxi. If staying at Airbnb ask your host if a pickup from the trail is available.

Day 2: From Tel Katz'a to Mt. Bental - 18 km

Maps: G2, G3. Water 4 liters. Refill available in Buq'ata gas station (off the trail). The gate of Kibbutz Merom Golan closes at dark and re-opens at 05:00.

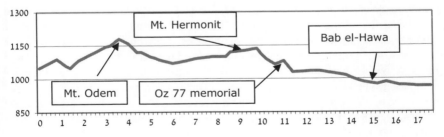

Start the day by Highway 98 on the ancient road at the foot of Tel Katz'a (0.0, 1050). Hike on a blue trail. At a trails' junction (0.4, 1070), turn right to a narrower road. **The trail enters the Odem forest, a remnant of the large forest that covered the Golan until about 100 years ago. It was cut down by the Ottomans for construction and commercial purposes. Various types of oak and other trees are common here. The trees are covered with climbing plants such as Italian honeysuckle and rough bindweed. The flowers are characteristic of high areas, and here you can find the Iris Histrio, Greek cyclamen and rare orchids. The fauna in the forest is plentiful; you can see rabbits, foxes, jackals, porcupines, wild boars and many birds such as short-eared owls, tawny owls, Syrian woodpeckers and others. An interesting geological phenomenon in the forest is the more than 20 jubas or pits created by gas eruptions during volcanic activity. It is difficult to see a juba because its edges are at surface level and covered with vegetation. The diameter of the largest juba in the forest is about 200 m and its' depth is about 50 m.**

Exit the forest (0.8, 1090) and continue straight on a mild descent. On your right there is a cherry orchard. The blue trail ends. A red trail comes from the right, continue straight on the red trail. Arrive at a road (1.4, 1050) and turn left on a mild ascent among cherry groves and apples. At a fork (1.7, 1080) turn right and climbs Mt. Odem. Pass by an old quarry on your left (3.2, 1150). At a trails' crossing the red trail continues to Odem. Turn left and reach the top of the ascent (3.6, 1180). **Mt. Odem is named for its red color (adom - Hebrew for red). Its Arabic name is Ras al-Ahmar. It is an extinct volcano with layers of volcanic rocks and pyroclastic materials in various shades of red and purple scoria. On its summit is an IDF post which is generally unmanned, in accordance with the 1974 separation of forces agreement between Syria and Israel. The view is spectacular: the Hermon to the northeast, Buqata on the east, and the Odem Forest a few dozen meters below.**

Continue downhill and pass by an abandoned Scoria quarry (4.1, 1160). **The word Scoria means rust in Greek. The colors were created as a result of thousands of years of oxidation processes.** Pass an iron gate and on your left, there is a container that has been converted for agricultural use as a storage room. At a dirt roads' junction turn left (4.4, 1120). Pass a cattle grid and further along the trail by a cowshed. Turn right, and cross another cattle grid (4.6, 1120), turn right at a fork and continue a mild descent. After ~200 m turn left at a trails' intersection (5.0, 1100) on a mild ascent. Pass among oak trees and continue on a slight descent. Turn left and pass a gate in a cattle fence (6.1, 1070). Pass on your left by a seasonal cowshed (6.6, 1080). The trail turns slightly to the left near the pine and cypress tress. Pass another gate in a cattle fence (7.0, 1090). The dirt road goes left and we continue straight (7.5, 1100). Route 98 is ahead of you. The Golan Trail turns left into a pine tree grove and arrives at the memorial of the 7th Brigade commando squad (7.8, 1100). **The memorial commemorates the soldiers who fell during the Yom Kippur war in October 1973.** *Behind the memorial there are picnic tables and you can spend the night here. There is no water. In Buq'ata (~1 km to the north) you can buy water and food; Kibbutz Elrom is ~1 km south of the monument.*

Cross Highway 98 and continue east on a dirt road to Mt. Hermonit. Pass by cypress trees (8.3, 1100). At a junction turn left (8.5, 1110). Mt. Hermon is visible to the north. Pass a cattle grid (8.7, 1120), and continue on a moderate ascent of Mount Hermonit. **The summit of Mt. Hermonit is 1211m above sea level, making it the second highest mountain on the Golan Heights. It is an extinct volcano, and the scoria is the reason for its red color. The name of the mountain in Arabic is Jebel a-Sheikha, meaning Old Mountain.**

Continue the ascent on the eastern side of the mountain. The trail turns left onto a steep descent (9.8, 1135). The view towards the valley of tears and Syria is spectacular. It's a good place for a short break. Arrive on a paved road and turn right (10.2, 1090). On your left is a turret of a tank. Pass an intersection (10.6, 1065) and arrive at the Oz 77 memorial (11.0, 1080).

The memorial was erected in honor of the fallen soldiers of the 77th Battalion during the Yom Kippur War. The battalion was reinforced by tanks from the 88th Brigade commanded by Avigdor Kahalani, and charged with the task of repelling the Syrian invasion of the Golan Heights in this area. The Israeli force, which numbered only a few dozen tanks, was deployed in positions that dominated the valley east of Mt. Hermonit, facing hundreds of tanks of the Syrian 7th Division. For four days and three nights the Israeli tanks held their posts, and with courage and determination they withstood the waves of Syrian attacks. In the decisive moment Lt. Col. Avigdor Kahalani managed to push his soldiers to a supreme effort, despite their numerical inferiority and the intensity of the fire - an effort that caused the Syrians to withdraw, leaving behind hundreds of damaged tanks. This victory marked the turning point of the war, giving Israel the opportunity to launch a counterattack that brought the IDF to the outskirts of Damascus. During the fighting Avigdor Kahalani called it the Battle of the Valley of Tears, telling his soldiers: "This will be the valley of tears for the Syrians". For his courage and determination Lt. Col. Kahalani received the Medal of Valor. It is the

highest decoration in the IDF, awarded by the defense minister on the chief of staff's recommendation for "a supreme act of heroism, carried out in times of war against the enemy." In 1970 the Medal of Valor replaced the Hero of Israel medal, which was only awarded in the War of Independence. Everyone who was decorated with the Hero of Israel medal automatically received the Medal of Valor. Overall, 40 medals have been awarded.

Go down next to a small amphitheater towards a stream which joins further to the east, Wadi Marja a-Shabrak and the Rockad River in Syria. Cross the wadi (11.3, 1030), turn left and continue hiking east. In the winter after heavy rains or during the melting of the snow, floods are common here. Leave the wadi, turn right and climb onto a narrow road (11.7, 1030). Make a left turn onto a dirt road at (12.0, 1030). Pass a cattle grid, and continue south between orchards. Turn right (12.2, 1035) onto an asphalt road at a crossroads next to the fruit harvesting facility. At the end of the cypress trees, turn left onto an ancient Roman road paved with basalt stones (12.6, 1035). On your right are Ein Hawar and Khirbet Huwara, and on your left are signs of "precautionary mines". Pass along an anti-tank ditch (13.7, 1020), cross a number of fences and cattle gates, arrive to Route 98 (14.6, 985) and cross it (15.2, 975). Climb a dirt road to Bab al-Hawa.

The place is called Bab al-Hawa (Gate of the Winds) because of the strong western winds that blow here. In the 1980s relics from the Iron Age, the Early Roman Age and the Byzantine period were found here, as well as crosses that indicate a Christian settlement. The findings from the earliest periods are rather poor, and indicate that the area developed in the Byzantine period mainly because of its location on the Via Maris between Damascus and Egypt. A Byzantine burial cave was also found, divided into rooms with basalt walls. There was also a tiny room for the burial of a baby. The oldest findings indicate an ancient settlement of the Itureans, who were semi-nomadic. They ruled the northern Golan in the second century BCE. Jetur is mentioned in Genesis chapter 25 as the son of Ishmael.

Turn left (15.7, 980) and go down towards road 959. By the road turn right (16.2, 970). Continue parallel to the road. The Bental reservoir is seen to our left. **The reservoir drains rainwater from streams flowing eastward towards the Quneitra Valley**. Cross the road, pass through a gate, and turn left on a dirt road that becomes paved. Arrive at a trails' crossing (17.5, 965). A right turn leads to Kibbutz Merom Golan, which is about half a kilometer to the west. Wild camping in the area is allowed.

Day 3: From Mt. Bental to Alonei Habashan - 21 km

Map: G3, G4. 20 km on the GT + 1 km off the trail to Alonei Habashan. Water 4 liters, refill available in Ein Zivan. <u>Bikers</u>: Detours by Mt. Bental and Mt. Hozek.

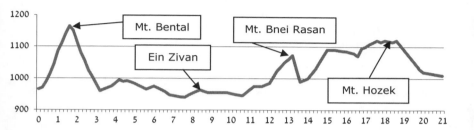

Start the day by the Bental reservoir (0.0, 965). The GT leaves the paved road (0.2, 965) and turns right into a trail with red markings. Pass a small dirt embankment and turn left onto a moderate ascent that becomes steep. We reach a fence that surrounds the water tower of Kibbutz Merom Golan (0.7, 1025) with a beautiful observation point on the kibbutz. **Kibbutz Merom Golan was the first Israeli settlement on the Golan Heights. In July 1967, after the six-day war, they have settled in a Syrian military abandoned military camp by the city of Quneitra. Following repeated shelling by the Syrians, the kibbutz moved in 1972 to its current location.** Turn left along the fence and start a steep ascent. Reach a dirt road (0.8, 1045) and turn left. After about thirty meters turn right to another steep but a short ascent. Pass by a locked bunker on your left (1.3, 1130) and after a few hundred meters arrive at the end of the climb (1.6, 1165). Turn left to reach Coffee Anan - The Cloud coffee shop. **Its' name is due to numerous cloudy (Anan in Hebrew means cloud) days in winter, but also reminds of Kofi Annan the former UN secretary-general.**   From the top of Mt. Bental (1171 m) there is a great view of the Quneitra Valley. Take a break here.

Next to the restaurant are a few sculptures created by Joop de Jung, an artist who was born in the Netherlands (1951) and has been a member of Merom Golan since 1973. De Jung usually uses scrap metal for his

artwork. The display on Mt. Bental is only a small part of his early output, most of which is displayed in Merom Golan and in his workshop. Mount Bental and Mount Avital to the south, are two parts of the same extinct volcano. Their names are derived from the Arab name of Mount Avital: Abu a-Nada - "the father of dew". The Arabic name of Mount Bental is Tel el-Bar'm, meaning the mountain which one goes around, because of its round shape. The Hebrew name implies that Bental - Son of Tal, is the lower one. Mt. Avital – Father of Tal, is 1,204 m high. To the east you can see the valley of Quneitra. The old city was abandoned after the Six-Day War and the new city of Quneitra was built to the east of the former city. To the west you can see (by the parking lot) the Star Junction at the bottom of the mountain. Mt. Avital and the volcano crater are south of the observation point.

The trail turns right toward the parking lot and crosses it. Don't go down the paved road. We reach and old military outpost (1.9, 1155). At the bottom you can see the Star junction. Go down a very steep descent, cross the access road to the mountain (2.3, 1105) and continue steeply downhill. The GT turns right into a small grove (2.6, 1025), and arrives at a road (2.8, 1005). Cross it, pass a cattle gate, and turn left on a dirt road along a power line. Pass a cattle grid (3.2, 960). At the Star junction (3.7, 975), route 9881 goes west to kibbutz Ortal and straight to Mt. Avital. The Golan Trail goes in between. Pass another cattle gate (3.8, 975), and after about thirty meters you reach a pipeline; Turn left and walk along it. In spring high vegetation hides the markers of the GT along the pipe. Pass over an old anti-tank trench (4.2, 995). By a pumping station (4.5, 990) there are two large oak trees. It's a good place for a break. Pass a cattle grid at (5.7, 965) and leave the pipeline. At an intersection of dirt roads (5.9, 965) turn left. Arrive at one more anti-tank trench (6.3, 965), and continue a mild descent among oak trees (7.15, 945). Cross a fence through a pedestrian gate (7.3, 945). Cross route 91 (7.6, 940) and turn left on a mild ascent. Arrive at the Ein Zivan camp area next to the Battalion 134 memorial (8.3, 960). There are picnic tables which makes it a good place for a break, rest and/or a night stop.

Battalion 134 was established in 1971. During the Yom Kippur War young soldiers fought alongside reservists and veterans under the command of Lt. Col. Hanania Tavor, together with other IDF units. Despite their numerical inferiority, they destroyed dozens of Syrian tanks. The battalion was disbanded one year after the war. Thirty-five of the battalion's fighters fell in the Yom Kippur War. The monument was erected in their memory. *By the entrance to the kibbutz there is a gas station* *where you can refill water. In the local grocery store you can buy food. Chocolate enthusiasts are encouraged to visit the "De-Karina" chocolatier shop which is about 300 meters from the gate. Open daily 09:00 and 17:00; Friday 09:00-15:00; Closed on Saturdays and holidays.*

Leave the memorial area and pass a gate in a fence. On the east you can see Mt. Bnei Rasan. On your left there is an old tank from the Yom Kippur war. Hike along a fence around an old mine field (8.7, 955). Do not cross the fence! Go through yet another gate in the fence and pass by an anti-tank trench (9.8, 955). Following a short hardly noticeable descent, pass by two eucalyptus trees on your right (10.5, 945). It is a good place for a short break and some historical notes.

On your north within the area of the minefield, are the remains of the Circassian village of Ein a-Zwan, after which Kibbutz Ein Zivan is named. Until 1967 there were 13 Circassian villages on the Golan Heights. The Circassians emigrated to the Middle East at the end of the 19th century, after Tsarist Russia occupied their homeland in the Caucasus and expelled most of them. The Ottoman Empire absorbed hundreds of thousands, settling them along the borders of the Empire in order to strengthen the grip of the central government and restrain hostile elements. This gave rise to fierce rivalry between the Circassians and the local Bedouins, who refused to accept the authority of the Ottomans. The Circassians established Quneitra around 1880, when it was a small Khan (Caravanserai). They also established the villages of Momsia, Hirbat Zarman (Tsurmina in Arabic) north of the Bashanit ridge, and Jouweeza. German researcher Gottlieb Schumacher noted that the Circassian villages on the Golan are different from Arab communities, excelling in their level of cleanliness and order. On the eve of the Six-Day War the Circassians on the Golan numbered close to 30,000, most of them residents of Quneitra. They have preserved their language and customs to this day. In the State of Israel there are two Circassian villages: Reihania in the upper Galilee and Kfar Kama in the Lower Galilee.

Continue east alongside fenced minefields and reach Highway 98 (11.3, 975). Cross the road and turn right onto a dirt road next to it. After a few hundred meters turn left (11.6, 975). After ~400 meters turn right and head toward Bnei Rasan mountain (12.0, 985). Continue straight uphill, arriving at the first wind turbine (12.7, 1045). **Mount Bnei Rasan, another volcano, is part of the Bashanit ridge. It is named after the sons of Ghassan, a Bedouin tribe that arrived in the region at the beginning of the third century CE. They converted to Christianity and fought alongside the Byzantines, who were** attacked by Muslim Arabs in the Yarmuk (636 CE). The Byzantine era came to an end after this battle, and the sons of Rasan became extinct. The ten wind turbines on the mountain were built in 1993. They supply electricity to about one third of the population of the Golan Heights. This project led entrepreneurs to plan the construction of fifty similar turbines on the ridge above Birqat Ram.

Continue south. At a fork, turn left, and pass by the sign "Mines". At another fork, turn right and pass an abandoned outpost. After about fifty meters you reach the top of the mountain (13.2, 1072). At a dirt roads crossing turn right and continue on a moderate descent. By the next dirt road there is a gate (13.5, 990). Turn left on mild ascent towards Mt. Curtham. **Curtham is named after the genus Curthamus. Safflower (*Curthamus tinctorius*) is a member of the genus.** Right of the trail is Hirbet Mumsiya. **Its' name was changed by the Syrians to Rassniya after the sons of Rassan.** Turn left at a T junction (14.6, 1050) and continue a moderate ascent. At the end of the climb (15.0, 1090) continue until your each another T junction and turn right (15.9, 1085). Go down the dirt road, and by its' end turn right. Arrive at a paved road (16.5, 1070), and turn left on a green trail. At the fork of roads (16.8, 1095) turn right; A left turn, is forbidden to civilians and leads to the summit of Mt. Curtham. Continue uphill and reach the top of the road (17.6, 1120). To the left there is an IDF outpost, where water can be filled <u>but only in times of emergency</u>. **As of this writing, <u>the access to Mt. Hozek observation point, is absolutely forbidden</u>. Do not pass through the locked gate to the observation point!**

Turn right and down. By a sign to Juweeza (18.6, 1120) cross a cattle grid and turn left. Go down through an oak grove and pass a short rocky section. Reach a wide dirt road (20.0, 1020). The Golan Trail turns left and you make a right turn to spend the night and re-supply in Alonei Habashan (20.9, 1010).

Day 4: From Alonei Habashan to Yonatan - 21 km

Maps: G4-G6. 18 km on GT. 3 km off the trail. Water: 4-5 liters. Refill possible in Keshet (off the trail). In Ein Fahm nature reserve the trail might be flooded in winter and spring, crocks or similar are required to cross a 30-50 cm deep small pond / large puddle. Bikers: There are few bypasses, please check the maps.

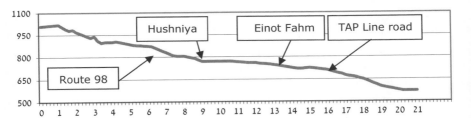

Start the day in Alonei Habashan (0.0, 1010) and hike east to get back to the GT (0.9, 1020). A green trail goes right to Ein Juweeza. Continue straight, and at a T junction turn right onto a mild descent. At a fork of dirt roads turn right (1.4, 990), and continue south-west. This section the trail might be flooded or muddy in winter and spring. Arrive at a paved road (3.3, 895), and next to the eucalyptus tree turn left. Pass by a water pumping facility (3.6, 900) on your right. The trail leaves the road and turns right onto a dirt road (3.9, 905), and goes south. A single tree is on your right (4.9, 890) and another water pumping facility on the left (5.2, 880). **East of the trail is Tel Sha'af a-Sindian (985 m), the southernmost of the thirteen volcanic mounds of the Bashanit ridge**.

After ~1 km pass a cattle grid and turn right (6.3, 870). Pass through a gate (7.0, 830), arrive at route 98 and turn left (7.7, 805). After ~200 meters, cross the road and turn right and west on a dirt road (7.9, 805). Pass a cattle grid and continue west towards Hushniya. On your right is the Golan Iris nature reserve. **The Iris blooms from mid-March to mid-April. There is a large concentration of the Golan Iris just west of the Keshet reservoir**.

The minaret of the mosque in Hushniya is clearly visible on the west. Pass by few eucalyptus trees (970, 770) on your left; In the winter there is a seasonal pond next to them. The abandoned buildings of the village of Hushniya are visible in a field right of the trail. Arrive at a grove of eucalyptus trees (9.8, 770). It's a good place for a rest and also spend a night. Wild camping is allowed. Route 87 passes ~200 meters from here, and the mosque is next to the road. The Golan Trail turns left and does not enter the grove. Pass a cattle gate, and continue south (10.0, 770). Tel Hushniya is located on your right side. Continue south along a fence and arrive at an anti-tank trench; In winter and spring the trench is flooded (11.8, 760).

Turn right and go through a gate, and a left turn follows. Climb the embankment above a trench. The trail on the embankment is narrow, pay attention not to slip down. Leave the embankment (12.2, 755) pass a cattle grid, and climb back to the embankment. Continue on the embankment for another half a kilometer and then go down (12.8, 750). Continue among old agricultural terraces passing an old large oak tree. Einot Fahm nature reserve is ahead of us. Pass a cattle grid and turn left onto a dirt road (13.7, 720). Hike along a fenced minefield and then pass a ford crossing (14.0, 720). When the area is flooded, water can be 30-50 cm deep.

Einot Fahm nature reserve contains dozens of springs with a significant flow of water. They are fed by underground water, and the flow is not constant. The meadows are rich in flora and fauna. Wolves, foxes and wild boars can be found here. Continue along a fence of a minefield on your right. By the end of the closed area turn right, and immediately thereafter turn left towards the eucalyptus trees (14.4, 725).

In the spring tall vegetation might cover the markers for several hundred meters. In such a case, navigate south-east to Hirbat Faraje. Go down through a tiny valley and continue among agricultural terraces. After about 1 km Route 98 is visible ahead (15.1, 725). Tel Fah'ress is visible to the south-east. **The Faraje pond nature reserve is actually a seasonal large puddle.** During rainy winters and springs water floods the area and a bypass is required. Continue towards Hirbat Faraje. Pass among the houses of the ancient village and after a slight descent arrive at a well, under a tree on your left (15.4, 720). Caution! The well has no fence around it. On our right there is a large building. **Ancient historic structures and the remains of settlements from various periods were preserved in Hirbat Faraje, including pottery vessels from the Roman period, and engravings of menoras, lulavs and etrogs. The lulav and the etrog are two of the four plants mentioned in the Torah as being relevant to the Jewish holiday of Sukkot. They attest to the existence of a Jewish settlement. Engraved crosses that were also found here indicate that it was a Christian settlement in the Byzantine period. Some of the**

buildings were intact, one of them containing a cellar intended for a goatshed, and there was also a perfectly arched roof.

Pass through a grove of eucalyptus trees, *which is suitable for wild camping*. After the grove turn right, cross a dirt road (15.9, 710), and continue in a small valley near vineyards. Arrive at a dirt road opposite a fence of a minefield (16.5, 690), and after 200 meters cross the TAP line road (16.7, 685). **The TAP line road went along the Trans Arabian oil pipeline constructed in the late 40's and early 50's. The pipeline carried oil from Saudi Arabia to sea ports in Lebanon.** In winter and spring, the road might be flooded.

Cross the TAP line road. Pass a cattle grid and continue along the fence. In winter and spring, the anti-tank trench on your left is flooded. Turn left and climb the embankment (17.0, 675). After a few hundred meters, the GT goes down and crosses the trench (17.3, 660). If the water is too deep (extremely rare event) you'll need to take off your backpack and carry it overhead. By a fenced minefield, and few eucalyptus trees on your left (18.0, 650), the GT turns right. Once again: if vegetation is too high it's easy to lose the markers. On the right there are the remains of a concrete small building. Continue along an agricultural terrace. Um a-Dananir is on our right. The Golan Trail turns left and after crossing a tiny wadi you reach a dirt road (18.1, 635). Turn right and hike west until you reach a T junction (18.8, 610). The Golan Trail turns left, there is a water faucet for hikers about 0.5 km after the left turn.

To Yonatan turn right and after a few hundred meters turn left and hike about 1.2 km until you reach the eastern gate of Yonatan (20.3, 570). The small gate is always open. The grocery store is located about half a kilometer from the gate in the village center (21.0, 570).

Day 5: From Yonatan to Um el-Qanatir – Ein Kshatot - 20 km

Maps: G6, G7. 18.5 km on the GT + 1.5 km from Yonatan. A hike to Natour adds ~1.5 km. Water 4-5 liters. By Mazra'at Quneitra you can refill water. Camping out by the end of the day: It is not allowed to spend a night in Ein Kshatot. You can refill water and camp out in outside the fenced area. You can continue hiking on the GT for another 3.5 km and camp out where Nahal Samakh joins Nahal El Al (day 6). Wild boars visit the place for drinking. Check for trail angels and airbnb in Natour (1.5 km east of Um el-Qanatir). Bikers: There are several bypasses for you. Check the maps and the hike description.

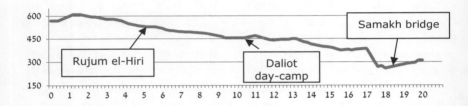

Start the day by Yonathan's eastern exit gate (0.0, 570). Hike east along the road. Turn right (1.2, 610) and rejoin the GT at a T junction (1.5, 610). At (1.7, 610) there is a faucet for hikers on your right side, continue south. The road turns right (2.5, 605), and we continue straight on the Golan Trail. Pass on your right a pumping station "Maayan Refaim" (3.4, 580). After ~300m turn right towards the eucalypti trees grove; The marker is on the first eucalyptus tree (3.8, 570). Pass another eucalyptus tree grove, and the GT curves slightly to the left. Turn right on a rocky dirt road (4.2, 550). Leave the dirt road, and turn left. Pass by a lone tree right of the trail. Rujum el-Hiri is seen ahead. Cross a dirt road (5.1, 530) and continue by a terrace. Pass a tiny creek and by the end of the terrace reach Rujum el-Hiri (5.5, 530) on your right side.

Until recently Rujum el-Hiri (The Ghost Wheel) was a mystery. It is constructed of three circles. The diameter of the external one is about 155 meters and the internal ~20 meters. The site was discovered after the Six-Day War by the Antiquities Authority. The only available information was its name on Syrian maps. The location was never excavated due to a lack of funds. It is not a biblical or a prehistoric site. In December 2010 Michael Freikman, a Ph.D. student in the archeology

department of the Hebrew University of Jerusalem, discovered that it was actually the grave of an important person. "The site is reminiscent of the pyramids in Egypt that were built as symbols of status. It gave rise to various myths, and when I started to work, I was apprehensive as if the site had some connection to aliens and the energy balance should not be disturbed. There are various theories based on pure imagination." Freikman adds, "According to a study conducted in cooperation with the Israel Geological Survey, the site has been in existence for ~5,600 years, dating back to the Chalcolithic period. In our study of the Golan Heights we have identified the remains of settlements and tombs from the same period".

Continue west and by an eucalyptus tree, cross a small creek and further west pass by a cattle pen (6.4, 505). After yet another cattle grid, turn left at the junction of dirt roads (7.15, 495), and immediately turn right towards the Daliyot water reservoir. Arrive at the Daliyot reservoir on its northern side. In winter and spring, fishermen spend a relaxing weekend here. Turn left (8.35, 485) and go down on the western side of the reservoir. Pass a pumping station and cross Route 808 (9.1, 465).

Cross route 808 and continue west along Nahal Daliyot. Cross a dirt road (9.5, 455) and continue straight and west above the impressive canyon of Nahal Daliyot. In spring red flowers cover the northern slopes of the canyon. At a dirt road junction (9.8, 455) turn sharply to the left, and arrive in the Daliyot day camp site (10.2, 455). The eucalyptus trees grove is a good place to rest or to spend the night. Continue on a dirt road with red markings towards Route 869. Cross the road (10.4, 455), pass a cattle grid and continue on a mild ascent in the field. Pass west of the abandoned village of Mazra'at Quneitra. Continue south and reach a crossing of dirt roads (10.9, 470). *About 150 m east of the trail there is a water faucet for hikers.*

Continue straight and south in a mild descent. Samakh water reservoir is visible ahead. Turn right (12.1, 440) onto an ancient Roman road that was part of the road connecting Damascus to Egypt. During very rainy seasons, water partially floods the trail. Bypass it on a more northerly path. Pass by Hirbat Rasem Balut, turn left (12.5, 445) and leave the Roman road. The trail passes over a narrow concrete barrier and continues south. Turn right (13.2, 450), arrive at a dirt road and turn right again. Hike on the left side of the Revaya pumping facility (13.8, 425).

Continue down the field and turn right. Pass between small water ponds covered in spring with water crowfoot (14.3, 410). Arrive to Nahal Samakh (15.0, 395) and continue along it. Reach a fence and pass it through a narrow gate (16.1, 380). Hike on the edge of a cliff above Nahal Samakh on a mild ascent. Turn left (16.9, 385) and go down steeply to Nahal Samakh. In the spring it is easy to lose the trail here in the tall thorny vegetation. In such a case, walk in the general direction of the bridge over the Nahal Samakh at the bottom of the descent. Turn left among raspberry bushes and following a right turn hike along an old fence (17.5, 305). Reach Nahal Samakh and cross it (17.9, 275). Arrive at a dirt road where you have a nice place to rest under the bridge (18.0, 260).

The basalt bridge was constructed by the Syrians in the 60's in an attempt to divert the water from the Hazbani and Banias rivers to the Yarmuk. The dispute over exploitation of the Jordan River and its waters began in the early years of the establishment of the State of Israel and has continued ever since. The conflict escalated when Syria established the diversion plant in 1963, leading to what became known as the "war over water." The work took several years, during which time the IDF launched air and land attacks on the mechanical equipment used to construct the diversion channel. The dispute over water was a major reason for the outbreak of the Six Day War on 5 June 1967.

Do not drink water from the stream without boiling it first. Cross the bridge, turn left and continue on a dirt road marked with black markers, which goes along the Syrian diversion canal. At a junction of dirt roads (19.5, 295) turn left. After about 200 meters turn left on a paved road and reach the spring of Um el-Qanatir (19.8, 310). There is a gate here. In order to enter the site of the ancient reconstructed synagogue (underline: recommended) you need to continue hiking on the black trail, turn left and climb towards the entrance of the site. It adds ~1 km. The site is open until 17:00 (fee). As of this writing the regional council plans to install an intercom to allow entrance from the lower gate too. Please follow the forum.

Day 6: From Um el-Qanatir to Golan Amphitheatre - 20 km

Maps: G7, G8. Water: 4 liters. Refill: Geshur (0.5 km off the GT on a steep ascent), Givat Yoav (off the GT), chicken coops of Neot Golan. In Nahal Samakh you can boil water for drinking. Crossing Nahal Samakh requires crocs or similar. By the end of the day there is no potable water to refill. Please refill by Neot Golan chicken coops at km 16.0 of the day. Bikers: There are bypasses for you, check the maps.

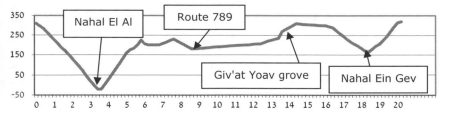

The Hebrew name of the spring Um el-Qanatir (Arabic: the mother of the arches) is: Ein Keshatot. Residents of the Golan heights call it the Rehavam Arches, after the late Rechav'am Ze'evi, a retired IDF major general and member of the Israeli government. He visited the site shortly before his assassination in 2001. Make sure to visit the ancient synagogue site. The remains of this synagogue were discovered by Laurence Oliphant and Gottlieb Schumacher in 1884. Oliphant's records indicate six pillars, three to four meters high, that were found in the rubble. In 1905 the synagogue was excavated by Heinrich Kohl and Karl Wetzinger, the archaeologists of the Galilean synagogues. Their brief excavation, lasting less than a week, resulted in a sketch of the synagogue. In 1932, the site was surveyed by Elazar Sukenik, the father of Dr. Yigael Yadin (the IDF major general who later became a famous archaeologist). Sukenik exposed the remains of a 14 x 19 m structure. Immediately following the Six-Day War, a survey conducted on behalf of the Israel Antiquities Authority revealed that it was a basilica from the Byzantine period, similar to that in the synagogue in Bar'am. The building was destroyed in the earthquake of 749, but the stones were not removed for secondary use, due to the remoteness of the site. In the summer of 2003 excavation and reconstruction was undertaken by Yehoshua Dray. The team mapped the stones with a high-resolution laser scanner and used computer simulation to obtain the data, which was logged into a database. Each of the items found was assigned an "identity card" that recorded its dimensions, type, direction of fall, location in the avalanche and more. The findings were marked with a miniature electronic chip, used to identify the position of the item in the original building complex. The building was reconstructed like a giant three-dimensional puzzle. The final restoration proved that it was a synagogue and not a basilica as had been erroneously assumed in 1967.

Among the findings were pillars adorned with an eagle, two ornate columns supporting the bimah (pulpit) of the synagogue and the pulpit itself, which was well preserved, along with the steps leading up to it. A menorah relief was discovered in 2007. The most exciting finding was the magnificent facade of the Holy Ark, which stood adjacent to the front wall facing Jerusalem, and which was preserved almost intact. The facade of the Holy Ark is richly embossed with vines growing from a vase, arches, geometric decorations and decorated cornices. The tops of the foremost pillars feature reliefs of the seven-branched candelabra adorned with Jewish symbols such as the four species. This is the only ancient synagogue where the facade of the Holy Ark was a separate architectural unit.

Ein Keshatot is located near the synagogue. Next to the spring are three arches, the largest of which is still intact. At the bottom of the pools non-local crushed chalk was found, of the kind used to bleach linen. This indicates that an ancient textile production plant was once located here.

Start the day by Um el-Qanatir (0.0, 310). Go down to the Golan trail. At the junction (0.3, 295) turn left and south on a dirt road marked in red. A green trail comes from the left (0.6, 290). Continue straight downhill on the red trail. The dirt road winds on a moderate descent. Pass a dirt road that turns left (2.0, 130), and continue straight. The descent becomes mild (3.2, 0) and you arrive at Nahal Samakh (3.5, -20) which is below sea level. When the flow is strong crossing the water here is tricky. The red trail ends at a fork, and you turn left onto a green dirt road. Arrive at the crossing of streams: Nahal El Al and Nahal Samakh (3.7, -20). Crocs or similar might be required to cross the stream. After crossing the water, reach a small grove, which is a good place for a break.

When exiting the grove, the GT leaves the green dirt road and turns left on a moderate ascent that becomes steep as you climb. Cross a dirt road (4.9, 140), and continue climbing. The ascent ends near the remains of the village of Adeissa (5.7, 225). Take a break here. The view of the Sea of Galilee is very nice. Try to wander a bit here and look for remains of a Roman aqueduct.

A short aqueduct was built some time in the first century BCE to convey water from the area of Kfar Haruv to Sussita (south of here, above Ha'on). With the expansion of the settlement, which at its peak numbered about 5,000 residents, two additional aqueducts were constructed, bringing water from Nahal El Al to Sussita. The length of each aqueduct was about 24 km and the height difference between them ranged from 5 to 18 m. The two aqueducts merged into a single channel at Sussita, ensuring a continuous water supply to the city, even if one of them was blocked. The first visible remnant of the lower aqueduct is a supporting wall at a height of 60 cm, found slightly east of Adeisa above the spring. It was documented in the 1880s by Gottlieb Schumacher (1857-1925), an engineer and archaeologist from the Templar community in Haifa. He conducted a comprehensive survey of the Golan Heights on behalf of the Ottoman regime, in preparation for the construction of the railway from Damascus to Haifa. At the beginning of the twentieth century he also excavated at Tel Megiddo, and published his numerous archaeological findings in a series of articles and books.

Continue the hike on a short flat section and then downhill. A dirt road turns left toward Hirbat Ta'eena, and the Golan Trail turns right (6.1, 200). Cross a small creek (6.7, 200) and continue on a mild ascent. Pass a fence and a cattle grid (7.5, 230), and walk down along the fence. The GT goes above route 789. Turn right, pass a cattle guard and cross route 789 (8.5, 180).

A detour along the roman aqueducts: Hike along highway 789 (Caution! Passing vehicles!) ~1.5 km and turn right and west onto a dirt road marked in blue, next to a brown sign "Ophir observation point"; On your left there is an olive grove. Hike west about 800 meters and at a fork of dirt roads continue straight for 100 m. Cross the fence to the right of the road, and hike down a few meters. The two aqueducts are clearly visible from here. The height difference between them is only 5 m. Follow the aqueducts until you've reached just below the Ofir observation point. It is worthwhile to climb to the observation point. From the Ophir lookout continue south on a blue trail with a great view to the west. After ~1 km, turn right and down and cross the aqueduct. Rejoin the GT at km 12.5 of the hike description.

Cross Route 789 (8.5, 180) and climb a dirt road with red markings. The Sea of Galilee is visible to the west (9.9, 190). The trail turns left and south. It is worth stopping for a break to enjoy the view. Continue on the red dirt road until it meets the blue trail that descends from Ofir lookout (12.5, 205). ~100 meters later, the red trail turns right and descends toward the old Bnei Yehuda. **Bnei Yehuda was established in the 1880s by Jewish families from Safed. The settlement did not last long and the place was abandoned because of internal disputes between the settlers. Some of the families were imprisoned in Quneitra following a tip-off that they were supposedly British spies. During the First World War only one Jewish family lived here. When the head of the family, Menachem Bernstein ("the informer") died, his wife and two sons continued to live here until 1920, when she and one of the sons were murdered by an Arab resident of the village**.

The trail continues southward. On your right side pass a few ruins, followed by a gate (13.4, 235). The ascent becomes difficult for about 100 meters and moderates (13.5, 265). Pass a crossing of dirt roads and continue on a mild ascent alongside the fence of an orchard. On your left there is a bicycle trail that goes around the Sea of Galilee at various heights. Giv'at Yoav is visible in front. The Golan Trail turns right onto a dirt road in a grove (14.4, 310). The grove is a good place to camp out for a night. *The distance to the village is about 200 meters. A grocery store is located at the main entrance of Giv'at Yoav by route 789, about one kilometer from here*. Continue south on a flat section in the grove. At dirt roads crossing (15.0, 305) pass a "minefield" sign on your right, and continue along the fenced minefield. At a fork of dirt roads cross a gate (15.8, 300), and the GT turns slightly to the right. Cross a cattle grid and turn right onto a dirt road. Pass by the Ne'ot Golan chicken coops (16.0, 300) and turn right on a mild descent. When the GT curves to the left, **stop for a moment and watch the remains of the lower aqueduct in Wadi a-Zeitun. On the western side of the wadi the aqueduct is clearly visible. Here too, a section of the upper aqueduct was discovered.** Do not cross the fences of the nearby old minefield.

Pass two gates (16.4, 290) and an olive grove on your right and arrive at a dirt road crossing by the end of a fence (17.0, 265). The GT turns right on a moderate descent to Nahal Ein Gev. Pass a gate (17.8, 195), and hike a short distance on a flat section. A large oak tree is a good place for a break (18.4, 165). From here continue on a moderate ascent. Pass by two gates at (18.5, 165) and (18.9, 200), and at a junction of dirt roads (19.1, 205) turn left and reach the road that goes down to Ein Gev (19.6, 265).

The GT rail turns left on the road, and after ~30 meters turns right on a moderate ascent. Continue on a dirt road (19.7, 285), and at the junction of dirt roads turn right and reach route 98 (20.1, 320). Next to the nearby Golan amphitheater you can camp out for the night. There is no potable water here.

Day 7: From Golan Amphitheatre to Taufik and Haon - 16 / 21 km

Map: G9. Water - 4 liters. Refill – Mevo Hama. The official end of the GT is at km 16. From there you need to hitchhike to your next destination. It is recommended to add 5 km and hike down to the sea of Galilee. Lease use public transportation which is readily available there. Bikers: There is a bypass for you from the Golan Amphitheatre. Map G9 north east.

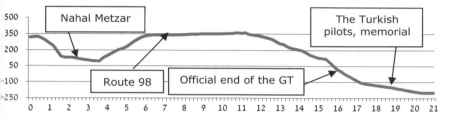

Side trip to the ancient city of Hippos-Sussita: If you want to visit the city of Hippos, consider several hours for the side trip. It is a 3 km hike in each direction, and a minimum 1 hour for the visit. Having said the above, it is worth the time. At the time of this writing the visit is free of charge. Go down the road at km 19.6 of day 6, and after ~3 km, turn right onto a black trail that goes up to Sussita. Return to the GT the same way you came.

The ancient city of Hippos-Sussita is located on the east shore of the Sea of Galilee, on top of a flat diamond shaped mountain, 350 m above the lake. It is almost entirely isolated from the surroundings with just a narrow saddle passage connecting it the western slopes of the Golan Heights. The ancient city moulded itself to the contours of the mountain, giving Hippos a rectangular shape. The entire city was surrounded by an imposing fortification wall. Sussita, or as known by its Greek name, Antiochia-Hippos, was founded after 200 BC, when that Seleucids seized the land of Israel from the Ptolemies. During the Roman period Hippos was part of the Decapolis, a group of 10 cities which were regarded as center of Greek culture in this part of the world. The excavation works on the mountain continues, and there are sites on the mountain that are still not accessible to the general public. Additional information about this fascinating archaeological site can be found on the web site of the excavation delegation: **http://hippos.haifa.ac.il**. You are required to leave the area before dark. The information is correct at the time of writing (January 2019).

Start the day by the Golan Amphitheater on route 98 (0.0, 320). Hike east and after ~400 meters cross the road (0.4, 325). Pass a cattle guard and continue on a blue trail. In spring the markers might be hidden in the nigh vegetation. The descent becomes steep (0.7, 300). Cross Nahal Barbara (1.5, 145) and turn left.

Note the limestone rocks characteristic of southern parts of the Golan Heights. Due to the type of land and the relatively low altitude above sea level, the vegetation here is similar to that of Mt. Carmel and the lower parts of the Galilee. In the spring, almond trees, cyclamen, anemone, and the common Israeli iris are all in bloom.

Pass by round rock formations (1.7, 130) that were created by floods; after ~0.5 km, Nahal Barbara joins Nahal Metzar (2.2, 130). Pass a cattle guard and reach a large oak tree, which is a nice place for a break (2.6, 115). Arrive at a rustic road (3.7, 120). The blue trail goes straight, and the Golan Trail turns right onto the road with red markings. The ascent is moderate but a bit long, some 4 km. Pass by an iron gate on the left (5.0, 230) and the road turns slightly to the left. The red trail turns right (6.0, 340), and the GT continues straight. At a fork turn right on a dirt road (7.7, 340) and arrive to route 98 (9.0, 350). The main entrance to kibbutz Mevo Hama is ~500 meters to the east. Turn left and continue hiking along the road. Turn right and cross the road (9.3, 350). The cemetery of the kibbutz is by a T junction (9.8, 350). There is water in the cemetery, like in any cemetery in Israel.

By the T junction turn left. Hike by a powerline (10.5, 355) and continue straight. On your right there is a popular paragliding site (10.7, 359). From 560 meters above the sea of Galilee, the view is great. Continue on a dirt road with green markers; at the junction of dirt roads (12.0, 330) turn right and continue on a moderate descent. Pass by route 98 and turn sharply to the right (12.6, 300). The trail goes down, turns left (13.2, 255) and continues straight. The landscape to the west is most beautiful. On a clear day Mount Tabor is visible in the far south. At a fork (14.0, 205) the trail continues on the right dirt road. Arrive at a meeting of several dirt roads (14.7, 155). The green trail goes right towards the

Sea of Galilee; Hikers who wish to end in Haon will turn right and continue the descent on the green trail. The description follows below.

The trail turns left (14.7, 155) by the eucalyptus trees on a moderate ascent. The trail curves right, crosses a cattle grid (15.1, 210) and arrives to Ein Taufik parking area (15.2, 215). At a dirt road junction (15.7, 200) turn left onto a good dirt road. Continue straight to the end of the Golan Trail by route 98 (16.0, 200).

To Haon and the sea of Galilee: From the dirt roads crossing at (14.7, 155), turn right onto a moderate descent on the green trail. On both sides of the trail there are mined fields behind fences. Do not stray from the dirt road. A sign points to Ein Sharir and we continue down. At (16.3, 0) you go down below sea level. Turn right at (17.3, -115) and arrive to the Turkish Pilots memorial monument (18.8, -150). **This monument was erected by the Ottoman government in memory of two Turkish pilots whose plane crashed in the region in February 1914, shortly after taking off from Damascus on their way to Jerusalem. The full story of the flight is inscribed next to the monument.** From the monument go down on a good dirt road alongside greenhouses and banana groves. The trail ends by route 92 and so does the hike (20.4, 200 -).

Turn left and after about half a kilometer you arrive at a gas station next to the entrance to Haon beach (21.0, 200). There is a fee to enter the beach. There are beaches where pedestrian access is free. If you want to join the Israel trail continue hiking south to Yardenit on the Sea of Galilee trail (purple markers). It is a 7 km hike. Alternatively take a bus to Tiberias. It has a stop by Yardenit. There are buses to Tel Aviv and Jerusalem too. Check in transportation.

The trail in 16 short sections

Below is a split of the trail into 16 short segments. The first section and the last one, are not part of the official trail. Very fit hikers have completed the trail in 4 days. Most hikers do it in 6-7 days. Please combine the short sections to set your own itinerary according to your preference. The numbers in parentheses indicate the day number in the hike description. Enjoy your Golan trail hike.

1. Top of Mt. Hermon to the official start of the trail (1H) - 4 km.
2. Mt. Hermon to Nimrod (1) - 6.5 km.
3. Nimrod to Tel Katz'a (1) - 6.5 km.
4. Tel Katz'a to the 7th brigade commando memorial (2) - 8 km.
5. 7th Brigade memorial to Mt. Bental (2) - 11 km.
6. Mt. Bental to Ein Zivan (3) - 8 km.
7. Ein Zivan to Mt. Hozek (3) - 9 km.
8. Mt. Hozek to Hushniya (3) - 10 km.
9. Hushniya to Yonatan (4) - 9 km.
10. Yonatan to Daliyot picnic area (5) - 9 km.
11. Daliyot picnic area to Um el-Qanatir / Ein Kshatot (5) - 9 km.
12. Um el-Qanatir / Ein Kshatot to route 789 (6) - 9 km.
13. Route 789 to Golan Amphitheatre (6) - 12 km.
14. Golan Amphitheatre to Mevo Hama (7) - 7 km.
15. Mevo Hama to Taufik (7) - 7 km.
16. Taufik to Haon (7) - 6 km.